This book was composed with Greylock's in-house Compugraphic Unified Composer editing terminal and Unisetter phototypesetter. Printing and binding were done by Whitlock Press, Middletown, New York.

The text typeface is English Times and the titles and headings appear in Paladium.

Chris Hansen designed the cover and the graphs.

EMPLOYEE OWNERSHIP IN PLANT SHUTDOWNS

Prospects for Employment Stability

Robert N. Stern
K. Haydn Wood
Tove Helland Hammer

November 1979

E W. E. UPJOHN INSTITUTE FOR EMPLOYMENT RESEARCH

Library of Congress Cataloging in Publication Data

Stern, Robert N   1948-
  Employee ownership in plant shutdowns.

  "A report to the W.E. Upjohn Institute for Employment
Research."
  1. Employee ownership—United States.   2. Plant
shutdowns—United States.   3. Producer cooperatives—
United States.   4. Industry—Social aspects—United
States.   I. Wood, K. Haydn, joint author.   II. Hammer,
Tove Helland, joint author.   III. Upjohn Institute for
Employment Research.   IV. Title.
HD5660.U5S73   301.18'32   79-23736
ISBN 0-911558-67-5
ISBN 0-911558-66-7 pbk.

THE INSTITUTE, a nonprofit research organization, was established
on July 1, 1945. It is an activity of the W. E. Upjohn Unemployment
Trustee Corporation, which was formed in 1932 to administer a fund set
aside by the late Dr. W. E. Upjohn for the purpose of carrying on
"research into the causes and effects of unemployment and measures for
the alleviation of unemployment."

This study is for sale by the Institute at $6.00 per copy for hardcover and
$4.00 per copy for paperback. For quantity orders of this publication or
any combination of Institute publications, price reductions are as
follows: 10-25 copies, 10 percent; 26-50, 15; 51-100, 20; over 100, 25.

The Authors

Robert N. Stern, assistant professor of organizational behavior at the New York State School of Industrial and Labor Relations, Cornell University, received his Ph.D. from Vanderbilt University. He is co-author of *Employee Stock Ownership Plans (ESOPs): Benefits for Whom?,* as well as numerous research articles in the areas of industrial conflict and employee purchases of companies.

K.Haydn Wood studied economics, politics, and labor relations at Monash University in Melbourne, Australia. He is currently a Ph.D. candidate at Cornell University.

Tove Helland Hammer is an assistant professor of organizational behavior at the New York State School of Industrial and Labor Relations. She received her Ph.D. from the University of Maryland, and has conducted research and published in the areas of leadership, work motivation, organizational careers and job mobility, and the effects of unionization on work attitudes and behaviors.

Foreword

Plant shutdowns have a potentially devastating impact on individuals and communities. Often the use of federal and state resources is required to reestablish employment stability and redevelop local economies. Social and economic costs of shutdowns are most apparent in small to moderate size communities where the local labor market cannot absorb the displaced workers and the economic base of the community is undermined by the loss of income. In some cases, workers and local residents have felt that the shutdown decision was an economic mistake on the part of the absentee parent firm.

This study examines the prospects of community-employee purchase of plants as one alternative to plant shutdowns. The authors analyze the costs and benefits which were critical to a decision to purchase a plant in one such case. In addition, they offer a methodological framework for evaluating community-employee purchase attempts in other shutdown situations.

Facts and observations as presented in this monograph are the sole responsibility of the authors. Their viewpoints do not necessarily represent positions of the W.E. Upjohn Institute for Employment Research.

E. Earl Wright
Director

Kalamazoo, Michigan
November 1979

v

Preface

Recent public opinion polls have shown that the confidence of Americans in the institutions of business and government is quite low. Despite the variation in opinion polls which may result from current short-run changes in the economy or world affairs, there is an underlying critique of these institutions based on their enormous size, power, and impersonality. Individuals fear that they have lost control over their own lives and futures as government regulates numerous activities and business acts according to an economic calculus which often ignores social costs and individual concerns.

The area in which loss of control is most apparent is the workplace. Economic and social welfare rest upon work in organizations which include labor in their decision making under the assumption that it is virtually equivalent to nonhuman inputs. The vulnerability of individuals to corporate calculations is never so clear as in the case of plant shutdowns. Few individuals are protected against a decision by a company to close a plant and move South or overseas. The company seldom provides assistance to anyone except top managers, and unions have not been aggressive in bargaining for provisions protecting members in the event of shutdowns. In small to moderate size communities, the impact of plant shutdowns may be devastating. The supply of local jobs will not absorb the displaced workers and the economic base of a community may be sorely undermined by loss of income. Individuals may be forced to move away to seek employment, and community life as a whole deteriorates.

In a number of recent cases of plant closings in small communities, groups of local workers and residents have come to believe that the corporation's decision to close was an economic mistake. Local groups have organized themselves to purchase the .plants which were to close and have saved jobs and preserved the quality of community life. People have sought to regain control over their own lives by becoming owners of the places in which they work and the companies which employ their friends and neighbors.

In the course of studying one of these cases, we became intrigued with the idea that "buying your job" was an act which countered the direction of American economic development. Rather than increasing centralization of the economy, local purchases of plants promoted local autonomy and decentralization of economic activity. We have undertaken a cost-benefit analysis of one of these local purchases for three critical reasons.

First, the purchase of a plant by local community residents represents the reassertion of control over personal fate by individuals who are ordinarily subject to the decisions of distant corporate decision makers. The effort to reassert this control takes considerable energy and has implications for the local quality of life far beyond the simple protection of jobs.

Second, economists, businessmen, and policy makers have tended to believe that corporate decisions to close plants are based on sound economic calculus and are not usually undertaken until all avenues of action are examined. However, such decisions are based upon examination of the monetary costs and benefits of a closing to a *company*—not to the community itself. If some threatened closures may be efficiently prevented by local purchases, community ownership must be evaluated in the terms which make sense to economists and businessmen. Thus, a cost-benefit analysis from the community's point of view is quite appropriate. The analysis should provide a methodology for evaluating the possibility that a company which a larger corporation could not administer profitably may be run successfully by locally based owners. Even if community purchases of a few threatened plants represent only a fine tuning of the system of capital allocation, a cost-benefit analysis will show whether or not such purchases are economically rational from the purchasers' point of view. When such purchases are sensible, they should be supported by business, banking, and government institutions.

Third, the analysis undertaken in this report should serve both as a model for evaluation of other community purchase attempts and as a tool to inform government officials who are in a position to support or reject efforts at community-employee purchases. Despite the historical existence of a great many cooperatives in the U.S., the idea of community ownership is novel to some and unnatural to others. Demonstration of the economic and social implications of these purchases may free bankers and government agencies from their hesitance to consider requests for loans and technical assistance.

As plant relocations become an increasing threat to the Northeast-Midwest industrial corridor, local actions to protect communities against economic and social decline become a critical necessity. Community-employee owned firms represent one possible local action which merits evaluation. When conditions are appropriate, this form of the reestablishment of local control over economic fate also merits a community effort.

Robert Stern
November 1979

Acknowledgments

The authors would like to thank the W. E. Upjohn Institute for Employment Research for its support and patience under Research Grant Number 77-04-06. Members of the New Systems of Work and Participation Program at the New York State School of Industrial and Labor Relations, Cornell University have also aided in this research through discussion, advice, and support. Ronald Ehrenberg, Paul Barkley, and Paul Schumann were gracious enough to read and comment on initial drafts. Sandra Heffron also deserves thanks for her effort in typing this manuscript. Above all others, the people of the Mohawk Valley deserve recognition for their self-help effort to salvage a difficult situation. John Ladd, director of the Mohawk Valley Economic Development District, Robert May, former president of the Library Bureau, Karl Vogel, president of IUE local number 344 and Earl Phillips, president of IUE local number 325 have been particularly important to this study and we appreciate their efforts on our behalf.

Contents

Contents

INTRODUCTION

1
An Evaluation of
Community Based Efforts
in Plant Closings

The March 29, 1976 announcement of the plant closing was hardly out of the ordinary. Sperry Rand's decision to close a small "unprofitable" subsidiary would not in itself make a ripple in the American economy, visibly alter the unemployment rate, or merit more than a two column-inch insert in the *Wall Street Journal*. Of course, the response in Herkimer, New York was quite different. Library Bureau, the largest employer in the three-town area, was to be closed which would further erode the withering economic base of the county. The Utica Observer Dispatch called the announcement a "blow to the area" that "hit area officials like a bombshell."

The American economy of the twentieth century has produced many such instances, contrasting the dismay of local residents with the routine disinterest of the national business community. The most recent announcement drawing national attention was made by the Lykes Corporation regarding its Youngstown Sheet and Tube subsidiary. In spite of some attempts by corporations to ease the local burden of a plant shutdown, communities are often devastated, losing jobs, tax revenue, and local sales, all of which weaken the social fabric of the community. In the Library Bureau case, however, the community response was far different. By combining capital obtained from the Economic Development Administration, bank loans, and a broad spectrum of community members, the plant was purchased and opened as a community-

3

employee owned firm (CEF). Rather than accepting the consequences of a decision made in a distant corporate headquarters, a grass roots effort was made to obtain control of the plant and save threatened jobs.

Such efforts, however, incur certain costs along with the presumed benefits of stable employment. The local population must organize a substantial effort, individuals invest personal savings, and local banks make potentially high risk loans. In addition, the federal government devotes a portion of its limited program funds to saving a plant in a small town. Any or all of these resources could be put to alternative uses, and the practicality of such an investment must be evaluated carefully, especially when a plant is to be closed due to economic inefficiency or lack of profitability.

The basic issue itself is easily stated. A business decides to move its production facilities or close them down and those employed by the company must make adjustments. Really understanding these events, however, is a far more complex and, in some ways, subtle problem. From the perspective of the national economy, inefficient plants should be closed, because capital must move to the place where scarce resources may be employed most efficiently. Social policy, including extensive transfer payments, has been used to buffer individuals from the externalities produced by the mobility of private capital. The labor market is supposed to reallocate work opportunities, and workers will follow the dictates of the market. Thus, from a system-wide viewpoint, intervention to prevent plant closure makes sense only when the closure is a miscalculation and actually reduces the efficient use of resources. At the same time, a social policy which obliged the firm to bear the costs of closing, rather than passing them to social welfare institutions, would result in a reexamination of the capital mobility question. What would appear to be a source of inefficiency now, would become an excepted parameter of economic decisions.

At the local level, the analysis is far different. Locally invested capital produces jobs which are the basis for local social and economic life. In large urban areas, the movement of capital is a commonplace event and larger labor markets have some ability to redistribute workers from single plant closings and to supply workers as new facilities open. Small towns and cities, however, do not have the same ability to reabsorb labor or to recover easily from the closing of a plant which employs a substantial proportion of the local work force. Capital which is employed inefficiently from an economy wide perspective is, nevertheless, critical to local survival. Thus, the political, social, and economic analysis of plant closings in smaller communities differs radically based on the level at which the analysis is undertaken.

This study is designed to look at the issue from both the system-wide and local perspectives. The object is a cost-benefit analysis of a particular form of local response to a threatened plant shutdown. It asks, What is the relative effectiveness of a community effort to purchase the threatened plant in lieu of traditional procedures for job relocation or retraining? Cost-benefit techniques are of course used with caution, both in light of the differences which occur across levels of analysis, and because several actual costs, avoided costs, and benefits are difficult if not impossible to quantify. What, for example, is the real cost of the reduced self-esteem which may be produced by job loss? After applying this evaluation technique to the community-employee purchase which occurred in Herkimer, the usefulness of the evaluation technique itself is considered. What information is needed to carry out such an analysis, and how readily available are the data? Is cost-benefit analysis a sensible approach to the problem?

Plan of the Report

The study is presented in three major parts. Part I considers the nature of the plant location problem in terms of community-industry relationships and the effects of a closing. Background information on the concept of a community-employee owned firm is developed and the specific case of the Mohawk Valley Community Corporation (MVCC) described. Part II evaluates the strategy involved in a community investment such as this through a cost-benefit approach. After examining the actual case, alternatives are considered and the difficulties involved in estimating both social and economic costs examined. The section includes survey results reflecting worker beliefs in their ability to find alternative employment had the plant actually closed. The results are used to modify initial estimates. Part III evaluates the methodology itself in terms of strengths and limitations, making suggestions concerning the utility of the cost-benefit technique.

In the final chapter, the community-employee owned firm is reexamined in terms of its ability to maintain local control and establish worker participation in the long run.

PART I

COMMUNITIES
AND
PLANT CLOSINGS

2
Communities and the National Economy: Decentralized vs. Centralized Control

Absentee Ownership and Community-Corporation Relationships

Social scientists have shown a continuing interest in the intimate relationship between industrial structure and community life. Beyond the local system of production, distribution, and consumption, a community's industrial base has been related to levels of income and education, housing conditions (Duncan and Reiss, 1956), occupational distributions (Galle, 1963), local political influence (Hawley, 1963) and levels of industrial conflict (Stern and Galle, 1978). The classical sociological studies of Yankee and Illini cities both demonstrated the influence of industrial organization on local social class relationships, and Whyte (1946) discussed the parallels between the status system in the factory and that of the community.

On the economic level alone, the mechanisms tying the community to its industrial base are manifold; the production process may require either raw materials or intermediate goods creating demand for local or regional suppliers, and employment opportunities provide income which consumers spend on retail goods and services. The industrial base also produces a tax revenue for municipal services and supplies individuals with the means to make charitable and civic contributions. However, the multiplier of benefits to a healthy industrial sector of a community also implies multiple levels of loss when a plant fails.

The existence of the industrial base ultimately rests on a series of location decisions made by those who control firms and who usually consider such decisions in terms of firm welfare and perhaps personal welfare as well. Form and Miller describe these initial location decisions in terms of comparative advantages in resources, labor, and markets. However,

> As markets grew, the tendency was to increase the size of the local plant and the labor force. With the depletion of local resources, the discovery of new resources, growth of national markets and the rise in educational levels, the relocation of plants to new areas became economically desirable. The shift from individual to corporate ownership helped overcome the force of tradition in keeping production centralized and locally controlled (1961: 71).

Stein reinforces this point by relating the stories of Newburyport, Massachusetts and St. Johnsbury, Vermont. In these cases the families which had built the companies providing growth and stability to the towns took an opportunity to obtain wealth which would be subject to little risk and require much less effort (1971: 31-32). The businesses were sold to other interests.

Warner extended the analysis further by looking at the precise form of the transformation of ownership which occurred in Newburyport.

> Two fundamental changes have been occurring concomitantly, in recent years, in the social organization of Yankee City shoe factories. The first is the expansion of the hierarchy upward, out of Yankee City, through the expansion of individual enterprises and the establishment by them of central offices in distant large cities. The second is the expansion of the structure outward from Yankee City through the growth of manufacturers' associations and labor unions, also with headquarters outside Yankee City and with units in many other shoemaking communities in New England and elsewhere. Both . . . decrease Yankee City's control

over its own factories by subjecting the factories or
segments of them, to more and more control exerted
from outside Yankee City (1947: 108).

Ownership passed to those whose interests in the location were
purely economic. The community itself became simply an
investment cost to the absentee owner and once that cost no longer
represented an efficient investment, the investment was with-
drawn. *Time* magazine reiterated the point with a recent report of
the study "Middletown III" by Caplow and Bahr (October 16,
1978: 108-109) describing changes since the classic visits by the
Lynds. "The local economy," they say, "is now controlled from
the out-of-town board rooms of large national and international
corporations—and from Washington."

On a broader level, such transformations of ownership
represent a major change in community economic life. Warren's
major theme in describing the "great change" in American
communities was the growth of extracommunity control. The
change "includes the increasing orientation of local community
units toward extracommunity systems of which they are a part,
with a corresponding decline in community cohesion and
autonomy" (1972: 52). Absentee control not only removed the
ability of communities to influence their own fates, but also
reduced their self-reliance in the political and social welfare
arenas.

The broad view highlights two other issues involving the general
integration of the economic system. First, cities may be viewed as
serving specialized functions within the overall system of urban
centers (Duncan et al., 1960; Kass, 1973). This division of labor in
production suggests that some communities will be tied to the
welfare of specific industries such as those in Ohio or
Pennsylvania which are tied to steel. Where a community is
specifically dominated by production in a single industry or plant,
its vulnerability to closure is particularly severe. Patterns of
dominance may provide a warning of potential future difficulties.

Second, the increasing integration of the economy is tied to
increases in production scale and the concentration of assets. This

increasing concentration has been the frequent target of social critics. Nadel (1976), for instance, points out that the 200 largest nonfinancial corporations controlled 60 percent of U.S. manufacturing assets in 1972. More interesting, however, is the frequency of corporate mergers and the increase in the types of mergers labeled conglomerate. Scherer (1970) identifies three waves of mergers in U.S. economic history. The first occurred around the end of the nineteenth and beginning of the twentieth centuries and largely consisted of horizontal combinations. It was followed by a number of vertical integrations and a few mergers for diversification from 1916-1929.

However, the most substantial and important in terms of the plant shutdown issue is the post World War II wave of conglomerate mergers. The development of legal constraints on traditional horizontal and vertical mergers is at least partially responsible for the shift in the dominant type of mergers. The Cellar-Kefauver amendment to the Clayton Act gave enforcement agencies the ability to challenge the traditional forms, and they did so between 1950 and 1970, but only 3 percent of the product extension form of conglomerate mergers were challenged. These mergers, in which both firms were functionally linked in production or distribution, but sold different products, became a strategic choice for avoiding government intervention. Likewise, mergers in the government's "other" category where the two firms had no common or direct relationship went unchallenged (Aldrich and Sproul, 1977). In addition, tax laws and accounting devices gave significant advantages to conglomerates for continued acquisition activity (Nadel, 1976).

Through 1968, nearly all of the firms on the *Fortune* 500 list participated in the merger movement. Most of them acquired small firms with under one million dollars in assets. The importance of conglomerate mergers grew throughout the period and, in 1968, they totalled 83 percent of all large manufacturing and mining firm acquisitions (Aldrich and Sproul, 1977: 3-4).

These conglomerate acquisitions have been accompanied by sales and liquidations at a dizzying pace. Accounting procedures which John K. Galbraith calls "creative accounting" have been used to assure that earnings statements present the impression of success. An FTC study has concluded that tax laws, especially those exempting exchange of stock from business sales taxes, create an institutional incentive for corporations to enter the acquisition and liquidation game.

Conglomerates and Plant Closures

The process of conglomerate mergers concentrates assets and economic power, but is particularly dangerous to those whose jobs are traded from owner to owner because the assets themselves are treated simply as investments to be sold at the appropriate moment. Often the selling comes immediately upon acquiring another firm's assets. The choice pieces are retained and the others released on the "big bath" write-off which Deborah Rankin (*New York Times,* January 31, 1978) described recently. When a new chief executive officer joins a firm, he may sell off weak assets to show his ability to produce results quickly. With only the best assets remaining, the company's earnings picture quickly improves. Though market forces are producing the closing of most plants acquired by overly acquisitive conglomerates, many such decisions are simply the result of corporate strategies which are only loosely related to production itself.

The issue is that these traded assets represent considerable productive capacity, jobs, and the well being of communities in which the acquired firms are located. Firms which might continue operation independently are closed once they become subject to the conglomerate's overall business strategy.

Unfortunately, conventional wisdom has suggested that economic nonviability is the central reason for plant shutdowns. Aside from declining product demand, major concerns are those which increase the costs of production in a given location relative to other potential sites. In the northeastern and upper midwestern United States, these cost factors have taken the form of high labor costs (often blamed on high degrees of unionization of the labor force), high taxes, energy costs and accessibility, transportation, and technological obsolescence. In numerous cases, federal regulatory pressure has fostered decisions to close down plants which were considered marginal or which corporate strategists viewed with ambivalence. Such regulatory pressure produced the decision by General Aniline and Film Corporation to close its asbestos mine in Lowell, Vermont, which was reopened as the employee owned Vermont Asbestos Group. Similarly, U.S. Steel had been wavering over the fate of one of its plants in Cleveland and decided to close it when faced with an Environmental Protection Agency deadline.

Conventional wisdom, however, usually hides as much or more than it reveals. These cost factors do not always appear together and are often weaker than news stories suggest. One Massachusetts study found that labor costs in the Northeast are not as significant a contributor to costs as press coverage suggests, but that corporations often move to escape the constraints of unionization. The study recommending steps which might be taken to retain industries in Massachusetts also suggested that taxes, transportation, and energy were real problems (Katz, Myerson and Strahs, 1978).

The critical issues in plant closing cases, however, are the degree to which closing decisions and divestiture decisions represent corporate misassessment and managerial priorities which result in the closing of relatively healthy firms or those which only require minimum investments and the appropriateness of the criteria used in the decision. How often are the cost factors either misperceived or used only as a convenient rationale for other corporate agendas? Though the importance of the failure of capital markets to allocate capital efficiently will be elaborated as part of the cost-benefit framework, several examples suggest that these "mistakes" occur with an alarming frequency, and that conglomerate, absentee owners are particularly given to such actions.

The narrow decision making perspective of many conglomerates produces weak commitment to any particular holding and considerable transfer of resources from one unit to another. Thus, decisions may be made to close a facility which result from general return on investment standards, mismanagement, decay of capital goods due to disinterest and the extraction of large overhead charges.

Rate of return requirements provide the most visible example of how profitable facilities may be closed by conglomerates. Chicapee Manufacturing, which provides 160 jobs for clothing industry workers, was receiving a return on investment of 12 percent. In other product lines, Johnson and Johnson, the conglomerate owner, obtained 16 percent and it decided to close the plant. Through a risk pooling arrangement, a group of 21 savings banks agreed to loan capital to former managers who bought the plant (Katz, Myerson and Strahs, 1978).

Bates Manufacturing in Lewiston, Maine provides a second recent case. The 1,100-employee linen manufacturing plant was part of a company which slowly became involved in the energy field and felt that the 7 percent return available in textiles was too low. This plant had been the initial holding of the Bates Manufacturing Company, but as the company diversified and became a holding company, the conglomerate psychology set in. A similar story is related by Stein (1971) in connection with the closing of Westvaco's Mechanicville, New York mill. Though closure was avoided in all three cases by sale to local interests, the conglomerates did not always cooperate in facilitating the sale and often seemed to prefer the closure, perhaps hoping to obtain tax advantages and in some cases to eliminate competition.

Purchase by local interests is by no means assured, even when the plant appears to be profitable. There must be an available, motivated organizer or organized group to press for the purchase. Many attempted purchases have failed for lack of necessary knowledge (Stern and Hammer, 1978) rather than unprofitability. It is not the case that all potentially profitable firms abandoned by absentee owners will be maintained by local interests.

The lack of concern shown for particular investments has occasionally produced corporate mismanagement and resulting firm decline and closure. The Saratoga Knitting mill in Saratoga, New York had been a profitable part of the Van Raalte Company, manufacturing high quality women's undergarments. After being purchased by Cluett-Peabody in 1968, sales plummeted from $72 million to $20 million a year, and by 1974, an $11 million loss resulted. Due to long distance decision making, the Cluett-Peabody office passed down decisions which resulted in inefficient use of knitting machines and disaster for the Van Raalte sales strategy. In the low margin knitting industry, these decisions meant substantial losses. One plant which was to be closed was purchased by local interests, including the employees, and is now running profitably. This study will show that constraints imposed by remote decision makers also limited the profitability of the Library Bureau subsidiary of Sperry Rand.

Conglomerates often exact corporate overhead fees from subsidiaries. This practice artificially reduces the apparent return on investment. In the Library Bureau case, this fee was substantial, as it has been in other places, and the general feeling among managers in the plant was that the parent company returned little in the way of services for the fee. Katz et al., described a meat packing firm owned by Ling Temco Voight (LTV) which controlled it through its Wilson Foods and Sporting Goods division. Scheduled for closing due to losses of over $1 million a year in 1976 and 1977, the company had lost much of its market due to increased costs imposed by Wilson. Beside overhead charges, the company had been forced to buy intermediate goods from Wilson at inflated prices (1978: 49). In still another celebrated case, the Colonial Press in Clinton, Massachusetts lost much of its market share under the management of auto parts and vehicle manufacturer Sheller-Globe, which controlled the company through a series of mergers. While reducing employment and ultimately closing the company, the absentee corporate owner extracted $900,000 per year in corporate overhead. Conglomerate owners lacking experience in a particular industry may manage to show a profit for their acquisitions at the same time that the value of those assets is reduced substantially.

The foregoing discussion is not an indictment of conglomerate acquisition and divestiture activity, but rather a statement of the problem posed for the communities in which the exchanged assets exist. As former Securities and Exchange Commission chairman William Carey remarked, "many of the rapidly assembled conglomerates of the 1960s have had to be taken apart at substantial social cost as the acquiring management proved itself inept" (*New York Times,* June 23, 1978). The problem is that communities, particularly small ones dominated by single industries or firms, are increasingly vulnerable to the decisions made by distant corporations over whom they have no control. These absentee owners do not need to consider the local effects of their decisions to divest assets through sale or closure.

The Employment Problem

While there is potential for less than optimal capital allocation decisions by absentee owners, the majority of closure decisions are probably made correctly from the owners' point of view.[1] However, the bulk of the costs generated by these relocation decisions seems to fall on the communities which lose plants. The workers whose jobs are relocated are often assumed to compensate for labor market changes by movement among jobs and geographic locations. This assumption is often unjustified. Those workers who are younger, skilled and less committed to their communities may be able to move and obtain jobs at comparable wages, but others, particularly the older, less skilled, and those with stakes in the community such as housing investments, relatives, or long term social relationships, are less likely to pick up and follow the shifting labor market. It is more realistic to recognize that labor market mobility does not adequately compensate all displaced workers, especially when opportunities are not available locally; opportunities are particularly limited in smaller cities and towns with relatively limited economic bases.

An examination of unemployment problems over time must be concerned not only with total amount, but also with the duration

---

1. There is no information available on the extent to which closure represents management miscalculation of profitability. This study will make clear the complexity of converting to worker or community ownership and the limited situations in which this strategy is viable.

and turnover components of unemployment. Turnover is a measure of the number of spells of unemployment or the rate of flow into and out of the unemployed pool, whereas duration reflects the length of time individuals are unemployed. Most analyses have focused on the importance of average duration, but the frequency of unemployment spells is critical to the question of local economic and social stability.

Several analyses have shown the importance of turnover related unemployment caused by plant shutdowns and relocations. James and Hughes analysis of employment location change in New Jersey concluded that "the picture that emerges is one of tremendous flux" (1974: 92). During just a two-year period (1967-1968) over 10 percent of the establishments in the 20-49 employees category either relocated or went out of business. Struyk and James, studying manufacturing employment in the Boston and Phoenix metropolitan areas, found that:

> The flux in both areas of establishment location and identity is enormous, even during the relatively short three year observation period. Approximately one out of four establishments operating in the two areas in 1965 either relocated or went out of business by 1968! . . . Even measured in terms of employment, the degree of flux is startling; over five percent of all jobs were involved in some "relocation" activity on an annual basis (1974: 51).

Twelve percent of employment in the central city of Boston in 1965 was in establishments which were defunct by 1968.

Mick's (1975) study of the social and personal costs of plant closures analyzed the 1954-1970 period for the rubber and plastic industries in Connecticut. The sector grew substantially—6,428 jobs were created by new plant openings. But, 4,634 jobs disappeared through 145 plant shutdowns, showing that even in relative growth industries, dislocations affect many workers. The rubber and plastic industries employed only about 4 percent of the Connecticut work force during the period and comprised slightly less than 4 percent of the state's total of 5,600 plants. Mick suggests that, if these figures are at all indicative of other manufacturing sectors in Connecticut or even in New England, "shutdowns must have been a constant problem with which thousands of people coped" (1975: 207).

Many of the older employment centers in the Northeast appear to be characterized both by high turnover in the labor markets, long lags in new job-worker matches, and by a net loss in jobs. Some writers have attempted to link job loss in the Northeast and Midwest to the increasing prevalence of multi-plant corporations, including multi-nationals. They suggest that a major feature of the complex of employment problems in older industrial regions is "industry shift" (Kelly, 1977). These analysts concentrate especially on apparent effects of absentee ownership and mergers.

Udell (1969), for example, gathered data on social and economic consequences of the merger movement in Wisconsin. The study emphasized the effects on employment and payroll growth rates. He claims that formerly independent Wisconsin firms which merged with conglomerate corporations had experienced significant decreases in post-merger compared to pre-merger rates of growth in employment and payrolls. Udell suggests that an important loss to the state is that merged firms tend to change to financial institutions, with legal and accounting services provided out-of-state.

Booth (1972) studied changes in employment for total manufacturing and for the shoe industry in Maine for both out-of-state and local firms. Over the period 1958-1969, for firms with more than 500 employees, the Maine firms increased their employees in manufacturing by 82 percent, and in the shoe industry by 110 percent, compared to the absentee owned firms' comparable figures of 8 percent and -12 percent.

Frank and Freeman (1975) have given an estimate, which they freely admit is "quite rough," that the U.S. economy lost 1,062,577 jobs through 1974 because of the activities of U.S. multi-national companies.[2] Organized interest groups opposed to

---

2. The jobs considered to be lost or displaced are those which would have been generated in the production of goods which the multi-nationals could have successfully marketed in the absence of overseas production of the same goods by their foreign subsidiaries.

this type of job loss also point to particular examples, such as the Ohio based corporations, Diamond Shamrock and Goodyear Tire, which have reduced their operations in that state and purchased a chemical plant and a tire manufacturer in Chile.

However, in general, these authors correctly note major methodological problems and are cautious in their conclusions. No firm evaluation of the effect of conglomerates on employment can be made from this type of data, especially from a societal viewpoint.

Nevertheless, it is relatively clear that, all else being equal, communities in which the major sources of employment are controlled by persons who have no crucial reason to give major weight to community-employee factors in decision making are more vulnerable to instability than in the opposite situation. The great vulnerability of communities whose economic base is dependent on one or a few employers has been documented repeatedly by company town case studies (Lantz, 1971; Strange, 1977) and dramatic stories of "town deaths."

Community Control and CEFs

The discussion has established a number of points upon which an examination of community control of industry may be based. There is an intimate relationship between industry and community. This interdependence was once contained within the local environment, but the nature of industrial administration has taken many decisions out of local control. Although a great many decisions to relocate plants are soundly based on economic viability, there are a number of errors in capital allocation which may result from the distance between communities and absentee owners. When these closing decisions are placed in the context of the difficulties created by high rates of change in job markets and the evidence of the apparent job maintenance which occurs under local control, the role of institutional mechanisms through which local communities may come to own or control industries becomes obvious. In cases where closing decisions are less than optimal or a little additional effort or investment may make a business viable, communities should be able to save jobs through a local initiative, including the establishment of locally based ownership. An option should be available in appropriate cases.

A community-employee owned firm (CEF) is one particular strategy which should be evaluated as a means of returning control of firms to local interests. Is it possible that CEFs can economically improve employment stability by reducing the turnover component of local unemployment?

A community-employee owned firm is a business enterprise in which the *employees* and members of the local *community* have a sufficient degree of *ownership* to ensure that the effect on the benefits received by employees and community members is given significant weight in (at least) major decisions of the enterprise and the opportunity exists for these groups to *participate* in making these decisions. "Employees" refers to those who are regularly employed or working for compensation in the enterprise and a majority of the employees should share in ownership. Following current practice in defining "community," (Warren, 1972; Hillery, 1955) the definition relies heavily on the notions of territory and function. The areas which supply labor provide a boundary such that " no area being analyzed should be smaller than that necessary to encompass the homes of most of the workers in the establishment(s) being studied" (Management and Economic Research, Inc. 1978: 49). Thus, those who reside within this territory, as well as those functionally tied to the plant who live within the area, are included.

An analysis of the CEF strategy should be concerned with the quality as well as the quantity of jobs which might be affected in comparison to alternative employment stability measures. Quality includes traditional variables such as wage level, general working conditions (including safety, etc.), and job security, as well as the job characteristics advocated by "quality of working life" proponents: self-direction and creativity (Davis and Cherns, 1975).

Quality of jobs also includes consideration of the impact of community control on area economic development rather than restricting itself to the provision of jobs alone. As a recent impact analysis of community development corporations has emphasized, different types of jobs have substantially different economic implications, particularly regarding multiplier effects (Block, 1977). Public service employment can lower the unemployment level quickly, but is often little help in providing long term productive jobs. For example, some public programs have attempted to increase job demand by encouraging tourism, but after initial employment increases in construction, there are minimal multiplier effects and much of the new employment is seasonal.

The employee-community purchase strategy should be considered in terms of economic development as well as jobs maintained. In areas with depressed economies, where plant closures and lost manufacturing jobs are a common occurrence, CEFs represent a targeted anti-unemployment program, and the need for targeting has been affirmed frequently in analyses of how unemployment might be reduced without added inflation (Dunlop, 1976; Gartner, Lynch and Reissman, 1976; R. Marshall, 1978).

An Illustration

Underlying the evaluation of community-employee ownership is the premise that CEFs may provide increased employment stability in a community. By redistributing ownership and benefits locally, a decision regarding plant location or employment becomes a matter of community political and economic activity. A decision to displace employees will give more weight to the costs to the community and employees than a conventional owner would give. Criteria other than simple business costs of profits would be given explicit weight in the decision process.

Though the major events which occurred in Herkimer are related in the next chapter, the manner in which community concerns enter into the decision calculus may be illustrated by an early board of director's decision. Soon after the Mohawk Valley Community Corporation (MVCC) purchase of the Library

Bureau, the company began to search for a new supplier of fabricated steel book shelves. The book stacks had been supplied by a subsidiary of Sperry Univac under a contract signed at the time of the change in ownership. MVCC was informed by Sperry that the contract would not be renewed after its March 1978 scheduled termination. The board decided that the most economical action would be the purchase of a small steel fabricating plant.

The result of the board's decision was the purchase of a plant in Vineland, New Jersey in October 1977. It is very clear, however, that the board gave significant weight to the community employment implications of its decision. The board was not only sensitive to community effects, but was also structurally tied to local interests since community members outside the plant held over 60 percent of the stock.

The first annual report states "although there are many old plants in our area, none fitted our needs as far as time and equipment were concerned." The board also explained that the local utility company was unable to obtain the required natural gas allocation and that the Vineland plant became available at a convenient time on excellent terms. Apparently, consideration of community employment was not a strong enough force to overcome significant economic advantages. The business decision was not sacrificed for community solidarity, but the community interest was given a hearing in the process.

At the same time, the decision to purchase a plant outside the local area produced criticism within the community. "Why hadn't the board paid the community back for its efforts and investment by expanding local employment?" There were phone calls, a few letters, and considerable "bar room" gossip. Following these episodes, the board decided to expand its membership to include two individuals who presumably represent community interests. The opportunity for community input into business decisions which is afforded by CEFs is apparent in this episode. Community welfare can be considered without necessarily jeopardizing economic soundness, but the criteria used in ordinary business decisions are clearly altered.

The Decentralized Control Idea

Interest in decentralized control over economic production and economic fate comes from a variety of contemporary and historical sources. Cooperatives in which each individual holds an equal share of ownership and and equal vote in decision making are the most well known similar form of productive organization. Jones documents the importance of the cooperative idea for British economic thought (1974) and examines the incidence of cooperation in the U.S. (Jones, 1977). Despite political and economic critiques of cooperative production by government, labor and management, Aldrich and Stern (1978) have been able to document the existence of over 800 such organizations in the U.S. over the past 130 years. Some were part of Utopian communities in which cooperation was an ideological basis for work, but numerous others were organized when economic conditions produced rising unemployment and depressed wages. Still others were formed as part of worker strategies to combat employers who refused to recognize unions. Some indication is emerging that the broad condemnation of cooperatives as economically inefficient was based on political interests and very little evidence (Aldrich and Stern, 1978). Cooperation should not be discarded as a philosophy of decentralized economic control.

Alfred Marshall is said to have remarked that:

> Producer cooperation is a very difficult thing to do, but it is worth doing . . . and . . . the difficulties of non-centralized cooperative production are just those at which it is best worthwhile to take a long pull, a strong pull, and a pull all together (in Pigou, 1925: 246).

More recently, a 1975 national poll by Hart Research found that 66 percent of respondents expressed a preference for working in an employee owned organization as opposed to investor or government owned firms, and that other opinions supportive of the employee ownership concept were widespread (see Rifkin, 1977). This form of local control may not include community ownership at the same time, but is a similar attempt to regain control of one's own economic fate. The incidence of employee owned firms is increasing rapidly due to ideas and advice on "worker's capitalism" provided by individuals such as Louis Kelso, and the creation of Employee Stock Ownership Plans as a result of favorable tax structures (Stern and Comstock, 1978).

Public interest groups, regional development researchers and political officials have given strength to the idea of local control and proposed a variety of strategies similar to the formation of CEFs. The National Conference on Alternative State and Local Policies and the Community Ownership Organizing Project promote more independently viable and autonomous local communities.

We propose, in short, that change in cities needs to be based on a program of community ownership—of real estate primarily, but also of utilities and even some businesses and industries. A city that owned itself—that was able to tap directly the income created by economic activity within its boundaries—would no longer be poor. And the direction of major resources would be in the hands of the citizens not, as now, in the hands of the largely nonresident managers and private shareholders (Kirshner, 1974:23).

Underlying many of these community control concerns is the notion that economic growth should be deemphasized, or at least that the social effects of economic and technologic change should imply real constraints on economic decisions. The popular conceptions that "small is beautiful," that less energy intensive and capital intensive types of development are now necessary, and that large-scale business and government are out of control, are also strong among those who advocate the more decentralized type of society implied if community-employee ownership of firms became widespread. Such advocates are also concerned with the lack of participation and industrial democracy under conventional ownership. They believe that a transformation in the control of property will increase the participation of employees in workplace decisions, reducing alienation and increasing individual commitment, autonomy, and satisfaction. The evidence from current cases of employee owned firms is as yet unclear on the existence of any of these changes (e.g., Stern and Hammer, 1978).

Questions of decentralized control and community or employee ownership have gained political attention. The Department of Health, Education and Welfare awarded $300,000 funding for a study of the feasibility of restoring a partially closed steel plant, in the Youngstown, Ohio area, to full production through a community-employee ownership plan. The partial closing has directly cost 4,100 jobs and it is estimated that an additional 1,650 to 3,600 jobs will be lost in other businesses because of the change in the area's income base and consumption patterns (Policy and Management Associates, Inc., April, 1978). The Youngstown study has examined the Herkimer case as a model, and has received considerable attention from the press.

Public figures involved in the Herkimer community-employee plant purchase commonly receive inquiries from communities similarly threatened by closings. The communities want to know how jobs were saved at the Library Bureau and seek an evaluation of the community-employee ownership approach. The president of the Herkimer County legislature dramatically stated to stockholders at the first annual Mohawk Valley Community Corporation meeting that "it goes without saying that . . . you have set an economic example through the State of New York and the entire country" (*Herkimer Evening Telegram,* January 20, 1978: 1).

In March, 1978, the Voluntary Job Preservation and Community Stabilization Act was introduced in the House of Representatives. The bill had 70 co-sponsors in November, 1978 and public field hearings were held in Jamestown, New York. The bill aims for an initial yearly funding of $100 million and is expressly designed to facilitate local actions such as the one which is the focus of this study. A similar bill is likely to be introduced in the Senate where there is strong sentiment on the part of Senators Long and Gravel to encourage employee stock ownership arrangements.

Legislation designed to reduce the negative impact from plant closures has also been introduced into the Ohio legislature. The legislation requires that all plants with 100 or more employees give (a) two years notice of shutdowns, relocation, or major reductions in force; (b) an economic impact statement from employers considering such action; and (c) payment by the employer of a sum equal to 10 percent of the total annual wages of the displaced employees into a "Community Assistance Fund." A Michigan state representative has proposed legislation which would require companies to give employees affected by a shutdown the opportunity to purchase the facility, before offering it to any other prospective purchasers.

Political rhetoric has begun to reflect the growing interest in these issues. Vice President Mondale has remarked that:

> It's time to focus on an element missing in the American economy—the right of workers, their families and the communities in which they live to some sort of decent treatment and concern when a company is planning or considering the possibility of closing (quoted in *Focus,* April 1977, p. 6).

Given the activity aimed at solving problems created by plant closings, concerns about unemployment, and sentiment for a decentralized economy, economic and social evaluation of CEFs is surely appropriate. Current measures to solve unemployment problems have not been particularly successful if the criterion of success is the elimination of structural unemployment.[3] While CEFs may reduce unemployment levels by promoting employment stability in themselves, they also complement other programs which have demonstrated partial success. They fit the pattern established through the creation of community development

---

3. Lipsey has defined structural unemployment as "that part of frictional unemployment which is not acceptable either because there would be a net monetary gain in removing it or because the social gains of removing it are judged to outweigh the *net* money cost of so doing" (1965: 215). Gordon (1967) says the concept implies: (i) some degree of immobility along one or more dimensions of the labor force; and (ii) in some or all of these sectors with impaired mobility, unemployment significantly exceeds available vacancies even when there is no deficiency of aggregate demand.

corporations (CDCs) which have been providers of employment under the Community Employment and Training Act (Community Services Administration, 1977). President Carter's urban policy emphasizes the failure of previous federal programs because the government lacked information to administer programs effectively. The new policy concentrates on local involvement and direction of programs such as CDCs in order to avoid the inefficiency of long distance federal administration. The original Humphrey-Hawkins legislation sought similar control over public service employment through local councils and boards. If CEFs are economically sensible, they will fit into other emerging programs aimed at combatting unemployment through local initiative.

This study focuses upon the ability of CEFs to avert structural unemployment particularly in the northeastern and midwestern United States where a syndrome of economic decline is in motion. The economies of declining regions are characterized by frequent factory closures, especially by multi-plant firms. There is a chronic lack of job opportunities, particularly jobs which match the skills and abilities of the unemployed and offer acceptable wages. Some of these communities and states are offering an ever increasing degree of tax and other locational incentives to attract and retain industry. But, these incentives are desperation measures because they are highly costly to current residents and industries[4] and even reinforce some of the syndrome characteristics. Tax breaks may attract industry in the short term, although state and local taxes are typically only about 2-3 percent of companies' costs and generally rank low as a locational factor (Weinstein and Firestine, 1978). However, the lowered taxes can reduce community services, school quality, and municipal viability to a degree which discourages industrial development. At some point the ratio of costs to benefits inherent in these incentive policies must become lower than the alternatives. There is an awareness among some groups in the Northeast, politicians and academic analysts, that such a point has been reached ("Federal Spending: The North's Loss is the Sunbelt's Gain," 1976; Bearse, 1977). Alternative

---

4. "Do States Neglect Old Plants for New?" *Industry Week,* July 4, 1977, pp. 43-49.

approaches are needed to break the syndrome. CEFs represent one such possibility which may be illustrated and partially evaluated through the events which occurred in Herkimer, New York in 1976, and resulted in the formation of the Mohawk Valley Community Corporation—a community-employee owned firm.

REFERENCES

Aldrich, Howard and Clare P. Sproul. "The Impact of Corporate Mergers on Industrial and Labor Relations." Working paper 26, Cornell University, September 1977.

Aldrich, Howard and Robert Stern. "Social Structure and The Creation of Producers' Cooperatives." Working paper 29, presented at the IX World Congress of Sociology, Uppsala, Sweden, August 14-19, 1978.

Bearse, Peter J. "Government as Innovator: A New Paradigm for State Economic Policy," in *New York State's Economic Crisis: Jobs, Income and Economic Growth*. Felician F. Foltman and P.D. McClelland, eds. Ithaca, NY: Cornell University, 1977, pp. 181-206.

Block, A. Harvey. *Impact Analysis and Local Area Planning: An Input/Output Study*. Cambridge, MA: Center for Community Economic Development, 1977.

Booth, Michael. *Ownership of Industry: The Maine Case*. Cambridge, MA: Center for Community Economic Development, 1972.

Caplow, Theodore and Howard Bahr. "Middletown III." *Time*, October 16, 1978, pp. 108-109.

Davis, Louis E. and A.B. Cherns. *The Quality of Working Life*, 2 vols. New York: The Free Press, 1975.

"Do States Neglect Old Plants for New?" *Industry Week*, July 1977.

Duncan, Otis Dudley, W. Richard Scott, Stanley Lieberson, Beverly Duncan, and Hal H. Winsborough. *Metropolis and Region, 1960*. Baltimore: Johns Hopkins University Press, 1977.

Duncan, Otis D. and Albert J. Reiss. *Social Characteristics of Urban and Rural Communities, 1950*. New York: Wiley, 1956.

Dunlop, John T. "Industrial Relations, Labor Economics and Policy Decisions," Presidential Address to the International Industrial Relations Association, 4th World Congress, 6-10 September 1976.

"Federal Spending: The North's Loss is the Sunbelt's Gain," *National Journal*, June 26, 1976.

Form, William H. and D.C. Miller. *Industry, Labor and Community*. New York: Harper and Brothers, 1961.

32

Frank, Robert H. and R.T. Freeman. "Multinational Corporations: Trading U.S. Jobs for Corporate Profit," *Viewpoint,* 4th Quarter, 1975, pp. 16-20.

Galle, Omer R. "Occupational Composition and the Metropolitan Hierarch: The Inter- and Intra-metropolitan Division of Labor," *American Journal of Sociology,* 69, November 1963, pp. 260-269.

Gartner, Alan, W. Lynch Jr., and F. Reissman. *A Full Employment Program For the 1970s.* New York: Praeger, 1976.

Gordon, Robert A. "The Aggregative Goals of Economic Policy," in *The Goal of Full Employment.* New York: John Wiley and Sons, 1967.

Hawley, Amos. "Community Power and Urban Renewal Success," *American Journal of Sociology,* 68, January 1963, pp. 422-431.

Herkimer Evening Telegram, January 20, 1978.

Hillery, George A., Jr. "Definitions of Community: Areas of Agreement," *Rural Sociology,* 20, June 1955, pp. 111-123.

James, Franklin, and J.W. Hughes. "The Process of Employment Location Change: An Empirical Analysis," in *Models of Employment and Residence Location.* F.J. James, ed. New Brunswick, NJ: Rutgers University, 1974.

Jones, D. "The Economic and Industrial Relations of Producers Cooperatives in the United States, 1791-1929," *Economic Analysis and Worker Management,* 1977, pp. 3-4, 295-317.

Jones, Derek C. "The Economics of British Workers Management." Ph.D. dissertation, Cornell University, 1974.

Kass, Roy. "A Functional Classification of Metropolitan Communities," *Demography,* 10, August 1973, pp. 427-447.

Katz, Carol, Jeanne Myerson, and Stephen Strahs. "The Policy Implications of Plant Closings in Massachusetts." Cambridge, MA: February 1978.

Kelly, Edward. *Industrial Exodus: Public Strategies For Control of Runaway Plants.* Washington: Conference/Alternative State and Local Public Policies, October 1977.

Kirshner, Edward. "Experiences in Community Control," *Work Force,* March/April 1974, pp. 19-24.

33

Lantz, Herman R. *People of Coal Town.* Carbondale, IL: Southern Illinois University Press, Arcturus Books, 1971.

Lipsey, Richard G. "Structural and Deficient-Demand Unemployment Reconsidered," in *Employment Policy and the Labor Market.* Arthur M. Ross, ed. Berkeley, CA: University of California Press, 1965.

Management and Economic Research, Inc. *Industrial Location As a Factor in Regional Economic Development.* Washington: Government Printing Office, 1978.

Marshall, Alfred. *Memorials of Alfred Marshall.* A.C. Pigou, ed. London: Macmillan, 1925.

Marshall, Ray. "Employment Policies That Deal With Structural Unemployment," *Monthly Labor Review,* 101, 51, May 1978, pp. 30-32.

Mick, Stephen S. "Social and Personal Costs of Plant Shutdowns," *Industrial Relations,* 14, 2, May 1975, pp. 203-208.

Mondale, Walter. "What Happens When the Biggest Plant in Town Closes?" *Focus,* April 1977.

Mohawk Valley Community Corporation. *Annual Report, 1977.*

Nadel, Mark. *Corporations and Political Accountability.* Lexington, MA: D.C. Heath and Company, 1976.

Policy and Management Associates, Inc. "Socioeconomic Costs and Benefits of the Community-Worker Ownership Plan to the Youngstown-Warren SMSA," Report for the National Center of Economic Alternatives. Washington: April 1978.

Rankin, Deborah. *New York Times,* January 31, 1978.

Rifkin, Jeremy. *Own Your Own Job: Economic Democracy for Working Americans.* New York: Bantam Books, Inc., 1977. (Hart Poll, p. 176)

Scherer, F.M. *Industrial Market Structure and Economic Performance.* Chicago: Rand McNally and Company, 1970.

Stein, Barry. *The Community Context of Economic Conversion.* Cambridge, MA: Center for Community Economic Development, 1971.

Stern, Robert N. and Phillip Comstock. "Employee Stock Ownership Plans (ESOPs): Compensation for Whom?" New York State School of Industrial and Labor Relations, Key Issue Bulletin, No. 23, Ithaca, NY, 1978.

Stern, Robert N. and Omer R. Galle. "Industrial Conflict and the Inter-metropolitan Structure of Production," *Social Science Quarterly,* 50, 2, September 1978, pp. 257-273.

Stern, Robert N. and Tove Helland Hammer. "Buying Your Job: Factors Affecting the Success or Failure of Employee Acquisition Attempts," *Human Relations,* 31, 12, 1978, pp. 1101-1117.

Strange, Walter G. "Job Loss: A Psychosocial Study of Worker Reactions to a Plant-Closing in a Company Town in Southern Appalachia." Ph.D. dissertation, Cornell University, 1977.

Struyk, Raymond J. and F.J. James, Jr. *A Comparative Study of Manufacturing Employment Location in the Boston and Phoenix Metropolitan Areas.* New York: National Bureau of Economic Research, Inc., 1974.

Udell, Jon G. *Social and Economic Consequences of the Merger Movement in Wisconsin.* Wisconsin Economy Series, No. 3, University of Wisconsin Graduate School of Business, Madison, WI: May 1969.

Warner, W. Lloyd and J.O. Low. *The Social System of the Modern Factory.* New Haven, CT: Yale University Press, 1947.

Warren, Roland. *The Community in America,* 2nd edition. Chicago: Rand McNally Company, 1972.

Weinstein, Bernard L. and R.E. Firestine. *Regional Growth and Decline in the United States.* New York: Praeger, 1978.

Whyte, William Foote. *Industry and Society.* William Foote Whyte, ed. New York and London: McGraw-Hill, 1946.

A Case Study of Community-Employee Ownership

The Regional Context

The popular press has made nearly everyone aware of the long-run economic decline of the northeastern sector of the United States. The snowbelt-sunbelt conflict in the "new war between the states" are two of the current labels. Most individuals seem to know the story of at least one company which has deserted the cold, old, energyless, highly taxed North for the warm, modern, energy rich, low cost South. As Houston and other southern metropolitan areas grow, the cities of the Northeast and Upper Midwest are pictured as blighted and decaying.

Behind the headlines is a picture of unemployment rates above national averages, net out-migration, declining numbers of manufacturing jobs in absolute as well as relative terms, and decreasing relative levels of per capita income. The related issues of population and job loss are illustrative. Net out-migration has increasingly cut into the population of the northeastern census area, particularly New York State (Sternlieb and Hughes, 1975: 9-10). While net white out-migration has been occurring since 1940, this trend was more than offset by in-migration of blacks. From 1940-1970, there was a loss of 900,000 whites accompanied by a gain of 1.6 million blacks. However, the outflow of whites has now increased considerably and the black inflow has been reversed. New York State lost 640,000 persons between 1970 and 1976 (Weinstein and Firestine, 1978: 5). At the same time, the southern census areas have reversed a long term trend of out-migration and showed a substantial population increase due to migration from 1970 to 1976.

Correlated with population movement are changes in employment opportunity, especially in the manufacturing sector. Though total non-agricultural employment rose by 70 percent nationwide between 1950 and 1977, it grew by only 28 percent in the Middle Atlantic States with New York trailing the group at 20.1 percent. Of even greater concern is an absolute decline of 6.4 percent in the total number of jobs in New York State since 1970. This state is the only one with an absolute decline in employment and contrasts sharply with the average employment growth of 37 percent in the Mountain States.

The location of the Library Bureau in Herkimer, New York is part of Herkimer County in the Utica-Rome Standard Metropolitan Statistical Area (SMSA). The principal cities, Utica and Rome, are located in Oneida County and almost 30 percent of the labor force in Herkimer commutes to Oneida County for work.

A rather complete economic history of the area has been produced by Crisafulli (1977) from whose work this description is largely drawn. Though the focus here is upon the industrial sector, the two counties continue to produce substantial amounts of agricultural goods. Oneida County is the third largest dairy producer in the state. Crisafulli's analysis shows that the industries which developed early and dominated the economy up to World War I hold only a slim position in the current economic profile of the area. Most development took place between the Civil War and World War I.

The single largest employer of labor was the textile industry which consisted of 72 firms with 18,126 employees on the eve of the First World War. This industry alone accounted for 43.6 percent of the area's total manufacturing employment (Crisafulli, 1977: 105). The industry was centered in Utica and relied on steam rather than water power, an alternative made possible by proximity to Pennsylvania coal fields and the transportation of fuel on the Erie Canal. The principal products that filled the canal's freight network were various lines of knitwear and other cotton goods.

Second in size and importance to the textile group was the metal and machinery sector. In the early twentieth century, this sector included 85 factories and employed 12,733 or 30.6 percent of all those employed in manufacturing. The cities of Sherrill, Rome, and Utica in Oneida County were the major centers of the industry. Utica specialized in the manufacture of guns, stoves, tools, and boilers. In addition, there were numerous primary metal foundries that catered to the railroad industry. Rome was the center for the production of copper and brass implements, while Sherrill specialized in silversmithing at the works begun in 1848 by the John Humphrey Noyes Oneida Community.

The third largest industry before World War I was the lumber and furniture group accounting for 2,245 employees or 5.4 percent of the area's manufacturing employment. Thirty-one such factories dotted the two-county area which had substantial forest resources, much of which is part of the Adirondack Park System today.

A fourth industry was "transportation and transportation equipment." This group consisted of all the ancillary services connected with the Erie Canal and the regional railroad system. The canal was finished in 1825 and Utica became a major warehousing depot for its commerce. A similar development accompanied the expansion of the rail system as Utica became the nexus of the rationalized New York Central Railroad with large freight and redistribution depots.

Two other industries were related to agriculture. The dairy products industry provided a stable element in the area's economy for nearly two centuries, and a second consequence of agriculture was the canning industry. Oneida County was apparently on the frontier of food-processing technology in the late nineteenth century. The Mohawk Valley agricultural base easily supplied this infant industry with a varied crop of fruits and vegetables. In 1912 there were 22 canneries in the area (Crisafulli, 1977: 103).

The current statistical profile of industry in the SMSA shows that none of the industries, save the metals group, figures prominently in the industrial mix. The earlier strengths are now on the periphery of economic activity and even the product mix of the metal-producing sector has radically changed (Crisafulli, 1977: 106). Though table 3-1 disguises this product mix trend because it shows steady growth for the metals sector, the massive structural change in the economic base which occurred in the interwar and postwar years can be seen particularly well in the death of the local textile industry.

Table 3-1
Distribution of Manufacturing Employment
Utica-Rome SMSA, 1912, 1947, 1976

	1912 (percent)	1947 (percent)	1976 (percent)
Metals and machinery.....	30.6	41.4	61.3
Other durables...........	5.3	21.0	7.0
Textile mill products......	43.6	19.0	3.7
Other non-durables.......	10.9	18.6	28.0

Source: Crisafulli, "Commerce and Industry," in *The History of Oneida County* (published by Oneida County, 1977), p. 106.

Although a popular local notion is that the decline of the Utica-Rome area was a result of the movement of textile firms to the South just after World War II, Crisafulli argues that the decline was actually in several industries and had been in progress for 40 years, but had been disguised by the economic stimuli of two world wars and the general decline of the depression. As the original industries declined, many dependent supplier firms and industries suffered. The decline then resulted from a loss of the local economic base in general. It was a long term decline of major proportion (1977: 106-112).

The transformation of the regional economy partially fits the pattern ascribed to post industrial society (Bell, 1976). The loss in manufacturing jobs has been accompanied by an increase, albeit a smaller one, in non-manufacturing employment. Manufacturing (at 32.3 percent of total employment in 1970) remains the basis of the economy, but employment in the non-manufacturing sector expanded by 28.4 percent between 1950 and 1970 (Crisafulli, 1977: 112). The largest advances were made in professional services, public administration, finance, insurance, real estate, communication and public utilities, and construction. A second development of the postwar period has been that government has become the most rapidly expanding industry, accounting for one of every four jobs in the area and having almost tripled its employment level since the end of the Second World War.

Table 3-2 presents an illustration of the devolution of the manufacturing sector, both in the durable and non-durable components, and the relative health of the non-manufacturing sectors. Lest the mention of "health" be deceptive, note that *total* employment in the SMSA in 1976 was 113,200, down 2,800 from 1975 and representing the lowest level in the 1970s (New York State Department of Labor, 1977). Tracing the employment levels in manufacturing through the table shows that the 1976 mark of 30,000 also established a record low for the decade, and is particularly noticeable in the "machinery, including electrical and transportation equipment" category. Both durable and non-durable manufacturing sectors declined steadily over this ten-year period; within the durable goods group "all of the loss came in machinery . . . once the heart, now the heartbreak of the local economy" (New York State Department of Labor, 1977: 4). This particular decline is considered the key to the economic malaise of the area, a situation exacerbated by plant closings and defense cutbacks that halved the record employment in this industry set in 1969. Major losses after 1969 occurred through the closing of the General Electric Radio Receiver plant, staff reductions at Griffiss Airforce Base, and the closings of Kelsey-Hayes Drop Forge Tool in Utica and the Univac division of Sperry Rand.

The precipitous drop in the last three years is partially explained by the nationwide recession, but it also underlines a general tendency toward contraction of employment in the manufacturing sector, particularly in this region. A critical weakness in the region's principal manufacturing component is also exposed. The

Table 3-2
Employees in Non-Agricultural Establishments
Utica-Rome SMSA, 1966-1976

(in thousands)

Industry category	1976[a]	1975	1974	1973	1972	1971	1970	1969	1968	1967	1966
Non-agricultural wage and salary	108.3	109.5	113.3	112.4	110.2	111.0	114.8	116.2	113.9	112.1	109.6
Manufacturing	30.0	30.9	35.2	35.0	34.1	36.8	40.3	43.3	42.8	42.6	41.9
Durable goods	20.7	21.3	24.6	24.4	23.7	25.9	28.7	31.2	30.1	29.9	28.7
Primary metal industries	4.5	4.0	5.2	5.3	4.8	4.6	4.9	5.1	4.9	5.2	5.1
Fabricated metals, inc. ord.	4.1	4.1	4.0	3.7	3.4	3.7	3.9	4.0	3.9	4.0	3.8
Machinery, inc. electrical and transportation equipment	10.0	11.3	13.0	13.2	13.5	15.7	17.9	19.9	19.1	18.1	17.5
Other durable goods	2.1	2.0	2.3	2.2	2.1	1.8	2.0	2.2	2.3	2.6	2.4
Non-durable goods	9.3	9.5	10.6	10.6	10.4	10.9	11.6	12.1	12.7	12.7	13.1
Food and kindred products	1.8	1.8	2.0	2.0	2.1	2.2	2.2	2.3	2.2	2.2	2.2
Textile mill products	1.1	1.0	1.2	1.2	1.2	1.2	1.1	1.2	1.2	1.2	1.3
Apparel and other finished fabric products	0.8	0.9	1.0	1.0	1.0	1.0	1.1	1.3	1.5	1.6	1.6
Leather and leather products	1.5	1.5	1.5	1.4	1.5	1.5	1.6	1.7	1.9	1.8	2.2
Other non-durable goods	4.1	4.3	5.0	4.9	4.7	5.0	5.5	5.7	6.0	5.9	5.9

Non-manufacturing	78.3	78.7	78.1	77.4	76.0	74.2	74.5	72.9	71.1	69.5	67.7
Contract construction	2.6	2.8	3.5	3.7	3.6	3.6	4.2	3.8	3.6	3.6	3.5
Transportation and public utilities	3.8	4.0	4.5	4.7	4.8	4.7	5.3	5.2	5.1	5.0	5.2
Wholesale and retail trade	19.9	19.9	20.3	20.3	19.7	18.9	18.8	18.6	18.4	18.3	17.6
Finance, insurance, and real estate	4.9	4.9	5.1	5.1	4.9	4.7	4.7	4.5	4.3	4.3	4.0
Services and miscellaneous	18.5	17.9	17.3	16.7	16.0	15.3	14.8	14.3	13.8	13.2	12.7
Government	28.6	29.1	27.5	27.0	27.1	26.9	26.7	26.4	25.8	25.2	24.6

a. Preliminary data.

postwar emphasis upon light manufacturing is particularly sensitive to cyclical fluctuations in the national economy. Recovery will always lag behind national developments since "much of the industry in this area acts to supply parts, or tools, for larger manufacturers elsewhere in the country. Before orders are placed with local employers, the inventories of the other producers have to be depleted" (New York State Department of Labor, 1977: 4).

Along with the increased employment in the government sector and services subdivisions, trade and finance have been fairly stable and contract construction, public utilities, and transportation have declined consistently.

The Labor Force and Unemployment

Population changes in the area have paralleled economic changes with high growth rates in the late nineteenth century and declining rates throughout the twentieth century. A sensible interpretation would have people fleeing a lack of employment opportunity. Table 3-3 shows the population of the Utica-Rome SMSA by race and sex for 1970. The grand total amounts to an increase of 9,899 persons since 1960.

Table 3-3
Population by Sex and Race, 1970

Race or Ethnic Group	Total	Female
Total...............	340,670	175,042
White	332,094	170,756
Black	7,686	3,818
Other Races	890	468
American Indian	249	124
Puerto Rican	613	314

Source: Annual Planning Report, Fiscal Year 1976, p. A-12.

Herkimer County's share in this total figure is 67,633 and is primarily located in that corner of the county near the industrial centers of Utica and Rome (New York State Department of Labor, 1975: 1-2). Whites account for 98.1 percent of the civilian labor force and 98.3 percent of the civilian employment for the entire SMSA. Blacks constitute 1.7 percent of the civilian labor force and 1.6 percent of the civilian employment totals. Only 62 of the 7,686 black males live in Herkimer County.

The Department of Labor has projected that by 1980, the population of the SMSA will decline by 1.2 percent or 4,044 persons. The decline is expected in the preteen age group while an increase is expected in prime-age workers (New York State Department of Labor, 1977: 12). Table 3-4, showing the percentage change in the population of Herkimer County for the twentieth century, lends support to the projection.

Table 3-4
Percent Change in Population, Herkimer County, State, Nation

Census Year	Percent Change		
	United States	New York State	Herkimer County
1900 - 1910	+ 21.0	+ 25.4	+ 10.4
1910 - 1920	+ 14.9	+ 14.0	+ 15.3
1920 - 1930	+ 16.1	+ 21.2	- 1.5
1930 - 1940	+ 7.2	+ 7.1	- 7.0
1940 - 1950	+ 14.1	+ 10.0	+ 3.2
1950 - 1960	+ 18.8	+ 13.2	+ 8.1
1960 - 1970	+ 13.9	+ 8.7	+ 1.9
1900 - 1970	+ 167.4	+ 150.9	+ 32.5

Source: Economic Profile: Herkimer County, Fall 1975, p. C-1.

The projection of an increase in prime-age workers will increase the number of individuals unemployed unless an economic turnaround is accomplished. The current lack of economic opportunity is harshly reflected in the SMSA statistical series detailing the characteristics of unemployment insurance beneficiaries. From 1970 to 1975, the percentage of males among those individuals claiming unemployment insurance (UI) benefits rose from 53 percent to 68.3 percent, indicating the progressively higher proportion of primary wage-earners in the jobless total. An analysis of age cohorts shows that the largest increase in UI beneficiaries has been in the 20-34 year old group (New York State Department of Labor, 1978: 43-44). Blue-collar workers in the SMSA were the chief UI recipients, accounting for 75 percent of total benefits for unemployed men in 1977. In conjunction with the general economic decay of the postwar years, Crisafulli noted that "The area has not known full employment more than a fifth of the years since World War II," and that "it has been classified as an area of substantial labor surplus for as long as these classifications have been published" (1977: 106). Herkimer County, however, usually runs a slightly lower unemployment rate than Oneida.

The income levels of manufacturing production workers have increased annually in the postwar period, but the increment has not always kept up with the Consumer Price Index and wages have been consistently among the lowest of the eleven SMSAs in New York State. The 1972 average weekly wage of a manufacturing employee was $185.72 in New York State; $167.32 in the Utica-Rome SMSA; $171.02 in Oneida County; and $160.10 in Herkimer County (Department of Commerce, 1976). Family income levels have also remained below statewide standards, and actually decreased in real dollars from the 1974 high of $15,540. The figures for April, 1978 show that the average production worker's weekly wage rate was $231.96, which placed the Utica-Rome worker ninth in the scale of eleven SMSAs in the state (New York State Department of Labor, 1978: 2).

Two other indicators complete the profile of economic opportunity in the two-county area. An analysis of quit rates for the 1970-76 period as a surrogate assessment of the workers general attitude toward the security of their employment and their willingness to risk seeking work elsewhere shows that area workers are becoming more tenacious and regard a steady job as a rarity.

The sum of these economic conditions must explain much of the unionized sector's inability to sustain work stoppages. Crisafulli attributes the short duration and narrow breadth of area strikes to the "statesmanship" of labor, however prosaic economic factors probably explain more of the phenomenon. While the Mohawk Valley has a higher rate of unionism than the national average, the number of workers involved and the number of man-days lost due to work stoppages has been among the lowest in the state and nation (Crisafulli, 1977: 110).

A final measure suggests the disparity in economic development between the counties of Herkimer and Oneida. Census data from 1970 showed that 28 percent of Herkimer residents commuted to other counties for their livelihood. Ninety percent of that figure commuted to Oneida County. The corresponding figures for Oneida County showed that only 4.8 percent of its residents commuted elsewhere, chiefly to Madison, Onondaga, and Herkimer counties (New York State Department of Labor, 1978: 12).

Economic Development Efforts

The principal agency in the area that coordinates industrial development schemes is the Mohawk Valley Economic Development District (MVEDD) which was established in 1965 under authority of the Economic Development Agency (EDA) of the federal government, an agency that was created under the Public Works and Economic Development Act of 1965 to "spur economic and social growth in economically distressed areas" (MVEDD Overview: 1). The MVEDD encompasses the five-county area of Fulton, Herkimer, Montgomery, Oneida, and Schoharie counties. In fiscal year 1976, the operating costs of the agency were approximately $105,000, more than half of which were covered by federal grants. However, the dollar impact of the agency's work was far greater.

The methods used by the agency are essentially two-pronged. First, it cooperates with local governments at all levels to help them acquire matching federal funds for infrastructural support to industry. These projects may range from establishing industrial parks to public works, including the development of transportation systems (MVEDD Overview: 2). All of these efforts are meant to attract industry, but there are also programs established through which existing private companies may apply for loans from the EDA or other sources to finance plant expansion or shore up failing firms. The underlying rationale in all of these efforts is the support for increased employment. Table 3-5 provides a rough approximation of the distribution of EDA-related loans and grants secured for the area by the MVEDD. Of this $17.25 million, $8.4 million was provided by local authorities during the decade.

Table 3-5
Projects Funded through MVEDD 1965-1975

General Project Category	Total cost (millions)
Industrial Development (infrastructure)	$11.7
Job Development (training and seasonal public employment)	2.3
Tourism	.9
Business Development (loans to private firms)	3.1
Planning (including feasibility studies)	.25

Source: Mohawk Valley Economic Development District: An Overview, part III, pp. 1-3.

The development of reusable industrial parks represents a redirected effort from the local development attempts of the fifties and early sixties. The Utica Industrial Development Corporation in 1957 attracted over 1,000 jobs in one maneuver by refurbishing an obsolete arms manufacturing plant in the city. Univac division of Remington Rand accepted the good faith attempt to entice them to Utica with a ready-made factory and stayed twenty years, until March, 1977 when the 1,000 jobs were lost through a corporate decision to close the facility (Crisafulli, 1977: 109).

While the MVEDD does seem to have injected rational planning measures into area development programs, the accomplishments of the agency have been dwarfed by developments that are beyond its control. The total impact, in terms of jobs, of the MVEDD programs in Oneida County during the ten years covered in table 3-5 has amounted to a gain of just over 1,000 jobs. In three months, at the beginning of 1977, the county lost that many jobs with the Univac closing. The task addressed by the MVEDD has been immense.

The social impact of economic dislocation is essentially immeasurable, however local legislators are annually confronted with the dollar value of their "social services" budget for the fiscal year. Those costs for Herkimer County alone have been more than 50 percent of the total budget in recent years and show no signs of diminishing (*Herkimer County Budget,* 1977: 42, 55). With a shrinking tax base and a relatively low property valuation rate, the economic viability of the area has been diminished.

Herkimer and the Library Bureau

Against this setting of regional decline, the announced closing of the Library Bureau seemed to reinforce the area's depression. The Library Bureau itself is located in Herkimer, New York and draws its workforce from the three contiguous villages of Herkimer (1970 population 8,960), Ilion (9,808) and Mohawk (3,301) clustered a dozen miles east of Utica. Of the 22,000 persons in the villages, approximately 8,700 were employed in 1970 with 80 percent of the jobs in the private sector and about 10 percent in manufacturing. In relation to the rest of the state, the population decline has been slightly more rapid and there is a clear dependence upon a healthy private sector for employment. A gross estimate of the economic situation is apparent in the 12.8 percent unemployment rate at the time of the announced closing when the national figure was 7.0 percent.

The importance of the Library Bureau to the local economy is apparent not only in the efforts (to be described) to save the plant, but also in the average age of employees (49 years) and average tenure (17 years). The pattern of low turnover which existed in the plant at the time of the threatened closure suggests that the 170 local employees were not easily employed elsewhere, in that they possessed specialized woodworking skills which were not consistent with other local manufacturing activity. In 1975, 650 workers in the same craft had been dislocated by the closure of the Standard Desk Company in Herkimer.

Corporate History

The Library Bureau (LB) is in the business of designing and manufacturing high-quality wood and metal shelving products and other library furnishings. The concern was found in 1876 by Melvil Dewey, inventor of the decimal cataloguing system, in an effort to improve library services through furniture and hardware improvements. Within its specialized field, the Library Bureau has prospered, selling not only standard products, but designing, supplying, and installing libraries in their entirety to meet the needs of educational and other institutions with significant or special collections. Library Bureau is reported to be the most respected manufacturer in its field. Its products can be found at institutions such as Notre Dame, Princeton, New York University, and at U.S. embassies and related agencies throughout the world.

The Library Bureau took part in several mergers from the time of its founding, and following the Second World War, relocated to the village of Herkimer, New York in a three-story plant erected at the turn of the century. It remained an independent company from the time of its founding by Dewey until 1923, when it merged with Rand Kardex, which in turn merged with the Remington Typewriter Company in 1927, to form Remington Rand, Inc. In 1955, Remington Rand and the Sperry Gyroscope Company merged to form Sperry Rand. Subsequent mergers resulted in the formation of the Univac division of Sperry which owned the Library Bureau. In summary, nearly half a century of independent operation was followed by a half century of control by outside owners, and finally after September 1976, the return of local control.

This small company has shown considerable success historically; one reason is its comparative advantage in being located close to its raw material supply. Close to half of its sales are derived from wooden products, such as shelving, vertical files, card cases, and larger filing and shelving systems. These products are manufactured from logs obtained locally and processed by the company in its own sawmill. Local farmers contract on an annual basis to supply the required number and quality of hardwood logs, for which they receive cash payments. These payments exceeded

$875,000 in 1975. The sawmill and plant house various machines for debarking logs, rough cutting, and planing boards. Further processing involves removal of defects, finishing, application of veneers, or thin layers of hardwoods, refinishing, and varnishing before assembly into the final product by skilled cabinetmakers. By processing its own raw wood materials the Library Bureau assures the quality of its final product. Only 30 percent of raw log material is actually used, 70 percent is resold to become pulp and mulch products. The annual cutting season begins in October and lasts through the winter. The sawmill did not process woods for any other purpose than supplying the Library Bureau until after the recent conversion to local ownership. By beginning to process lumber for local contractors and lumber yards, previously idle time has become profitable. While value is added to the raw material during processing, large inventories, annually amounting to $2 million, are required to keep the operation supplied. These inventories are a direct result of the nature of wood processing, which requires extended periods for drying and treatment.

A third of the Library Bureau's sales are derived from steel shelving products, which were until recently supplied under agreement from another subsidiary of Sperry Rand located in Ohio. Remaining sales consist of accessories subcontracted to other companies or bought outright and resold at a profit. An earlier, short-lived venture into plastic furniture items was discontinued when the company was unable to assure the quality standards it met for its other products.

A second important factor in Library Bureau's business is the manner in which it markets its product. When the company merged with Sperry Rand in 1955, it became corporate policy to sell its products only within the United States. At the time, this caused some consternation within the company, as planning had already been devoted to filling an order for the King of Sweden, who wanted a complete library installed. Furthermore, it was a long-standing company policy to sell only to those libraries employing professional librarians. This meant that the majority of its business was conducted with larger libraries, usually those supported by public funds.

With the cutbacks in federal and state spending that occurred in the late 1960s and through the 1970s, Library Bureau's market did not expand. If anything, it shrank. The company's marketing policies also meant that orders were budgeted and payments assured in advance of production. Customers made budget arrangements for purchases six months to two years in advance of expected delivery. This implies a very low loss on accounts receivable, but a vulnerability to rapid bouts of inflation. The company has had approximately 18,000 customers, and recent annual sales averaged $10 million, which amounts to a healthy 15-20 percent of the U.S. market, with a profit of 6-7 percent after taxes. As no single customer accounts for more than 10 percent of Library Bureau's business, the company is insulated from drastic short-run changes in demand for its product. The company's age and specialization relative to its competitors provides experience in estimating the costs of completing customer orders. Since sales largely derive from competitive bidding on open contracts, its experience and reputation are valuable assets. Nevertheless, as a result of the cutbacks in public spending described above, the company sought to increase direct orders. Under Sperry Rand, Library Bureau sales personnel were permitted to operate out of the parent company's marketing offices, but a rule was established limiting the access of Library Bureau salesmen to those customers not being cultivated by salesmen from other divisions of the conglomerate.

The Library Bureau employed (in 1976) 276 persons: 170 in manufacturing, 51 in administration and technical work, and 55 in sales. The production workers and clerical workers are represented by two locals of the International Union of Electrical, Radio and Machine Workers (IUE). Production employees receive payment through an incentive system based on individual productivity. Operations in the plant are arranged with highest skills (final assembly and finishing) being allocated to the upper floors of the plant, and lower-skilled operations to the first floor, sawmill, and log yard.

The manufacturing process is best described as a flow of materials from the sawmill on the ground floor to the finishing room on the third floor. Parts are placed on hand-trolleys which are moved among various machines. These machines include table saws, automatic assembly equipment, boring equipment, multi-head moulders, and edge-binders (multi-head refers to the capacity of a single machine to perform the same function simultaneously on several pieces of raw material). These machines are run by one or at most two employees.

Several of Library Bureau's machines are quite old, but practically unreplaceable. Normally, machinery depreciates in value over time, but the reverse has occurred with Library Bureau's equipment. These machines were manufactured in Germany and Switzerland, countries which have experienced favorable postwar currency shifts with respect to the U.S. dollar. In addition, importation taxes on such equipment have risen considerably. These economic factors, and the fact that the lead time for the replacement of such machinery is two years or more, give Library Bureau favorable footing against competitors seeking to enter the market.

The preceding account reveals a company with easy access to resources, a stable market, and a reasonable return on investments, based on conservative marketing. Nevertheless, Sperry Rand reached a decision to liquidate its holdings in this firm. Though very little information is available to account for decisions which were taken at Sperry Rand concerning the Library Bureau, there is information sufficient to suggest that Sperry had a marginal commitment to the plant regardless of profitability. Library furniture production was inconsistent with most of Sperry's activity and the return on investment available in this industry was below that of investments in electronic technology.

Community Crisis and Mobilization

On March 29, 1976, Sperry Rand made formal public announcement of its intention to liquidate its holdings in the Library Bureau and to terminate the division within twelve months. In the conglomerate's 1975 annual shareholder's report, a sum of $2 million had been allocated to financing the anticipated close down. From the sale of LB inventories, equipment, and facilities, Sperry expected to realize $7 million. Although the company's intentions had been manifest to local businessmen and others for some years, the public disclosure was described as a sudden event in the local press.

During the years 1972-1975, on four different occasions, Sperry Rand had been approached by two distinct groups seeking to purchase the LB. One group was made up of representatives of senior LB management and the other of local business investors. Though the general public's awareness had not been aroused, these locally-based efforts established certain contacts and crystallized interest in a purchase attempt among important members of the community, prior to the formal announcement of March 29.

However, the issue may not have been so clear to those representing Sperry. In 1974, the merger between Sperry Rand and Univac resulted in the new Univac division taking control of the Library Bureau. The process of merger may have affected managerial focus on the LB and suspended Sperry's policy making with respect to that division. By the time of the public announcement of liquidation, LB had become only one part of a general plan common to the merged companies to divest themselves of less profitable, older divisions, or those employing technologies less consistent with the major products of Sperry Rand. At the time of the announcement concerning LB, these plans had already shown concrete results in the closing of a Univac plant in Utica in 1975 and the announcement of intentions to close three more in the state.

In any case, the separate attempts between 1972 and 1975 by LB management and the group of local investors had not borne fruit. It is not known whether Sperry was approached during this period, or during subsequent negotiations, with representations by competing businesses or interests other than those arising from LB management or the community. Any approach of this kind might have had the effect of raising or lowering, in either case of fixing, Sperry's expectations with respect to what it could realize from the liquidation of LB, and would have affected subsequent negotiations with the local groups described above. Despite engaging in negotiations with these groups, prior to March 1976, Sperry had not committed itself to selling the division as an operating concern. Indeed, the March 1976 announcement spoke of a phasing out of operations and separate liquidation of the various LB assets, implying that LB jobs would be lost to the community regardless of whether offers were received for the entire LB operation. The issue of lost jobs and public reaction did not enter into the various negotiations prior to the announcement in March 1976 that the LB division would be phased out and terminated by March 1977.

Upon receiving word of Sperry's announcement in his Washington offices, Representative Donald J. Mitchell from District 31—which includes Herkimer County—attempted to sway Sperry from its decision. It is not known whether he attempted to influence the decision Sperry had taken to sell, or only the decision to close down the LB. Presumably, he was concerned that a closedown would affect employment, whereas a sale would only put the LB jobs at risk, under whatever policy the subsequent owners adopted. However, he learned that Sperry's decision was "irrevocable." Mitchell contacted Richard Rifenburgh, then in Florida on business, and urged him to contact Sperry executives, in turn, to further reason with them. Mitchell and Rifenburgh were co-chairmen of the Mohawk Valley's Business Assistance Committee, a group of community and business leaders formed to aid industry in the economically depressed Mohawk Valley. The committee had a continuing and special interest in bringing pressure to bear on absentee owners intending to withdraw industries and business from the area.

Rifenburgh maintained other interests which tied him to LB and the Herkimer area. He personally led the group of local investors which had, in 1975, made the most recent overtures to Sperry Univac to purchase the LB. His group had commissioned a commercial credit study of the Library Bureau at that time to determine whether the division's assets could be used through mortgaging to obtain sufficient credit to purchase the division from Sperry. While credit on these assets would have been available, the sum did not begin to meet Sperry's 1975 price of $5.6 million which represented a considerable drop from the $11 million quoted in 1972. This substantial change in asking price was due to changes in inventories and accounts receivable. Nevertheless, in June 1975, Rifenburgh's group had developed a financing plan, working through an independent Florida-based gasoline distribution company of which Rifenburgh was a director. The plan was based on commercial banking loans, federal loans (EDA), and public subscriptions, and contained the idea that employees and the local public would be independent owners of a new LB. This plan would surface again in 1976, following the Sperry Rand announcement.

Rifenburgh had formerly been a member of management in Sperry's Univac division; he had quit in the early 1960s to promote his own business interests. In 1976, these interests included ownership of Moval Management Corporation, director and officer of various other companies, as well as chairmanship of the 40-company Computer Industry Association. An early venture in data control systems financed with overseas capital culminated in Rifenburgh and seven others becoming millionaires. However, the company they managed subsequently suffered heavy losses in trading on the international money market. Although Rifenburgh was financially successful and held important ties to local business, his earlier entrepreneurial efforts had gained him a somewhat harsh local reputation as someone prone to taking high risks.

When Rifenburgh contacted Sperry Rand on behalf of Mitchell and the Business Assistance Committee, he received much the same response that Mitchell had. That is, Sperry's decision was firm: the plant would be phased out and the various assets sold separately. When Mitchell received this news from Rifenburgh, early in April, he arranged an emergency meeting between himself, Rifenburgh and others, and representatives of local, state, and federal agencies. These included the Small Business Administration, the Federal Housing Authority, the Economic Development Administration, the New York State Commerce Bureau, the Job

Development Authority, and the Farmers Home Administration. Those present expressed willingness to support a local effort to purchase the LB division from Sperry, but it was not readily apparent how a sufficient amount of equity could be raised to meet the terms of various public and private credit sources. However, the meeting led community leaders to doubt the inflexibility of Sperry's phase-out plans. Those involved worked under the assumption that Sperry would consider any offer that was made in good faith.

Following the March 29 announcement by Sperry, representatives of both the management group and the group of local investors (including Rifenburgh) reviewed their separate efforts to negotiate with Sperry. The only tie between these two groups, besides their common interest in purchasing the LB, was in the person of John Ladd, director of the Mohawk Valley Economic Development District. He had been advising both groups since their initial interest in purchasing the plant in 1972. Ladd had been approached because his non-profit organization, the MVEDD, had local jurisdiction under the Economic Development Administration to administer loan and grant funds to Mohawk Valley businesses and programs, and had the mandate and expertise to guide this kind of application to the proper agency officials. Ladd himself was a successful businessman, with ownership interests in several short line railroads and freight cars which he leased to large railroads. Most important was the respect which both groups held for his judgment.

The LB management group, headed by Robert May, the director of marketing for LB, knew the business well, but had little grasp of the financing problems involved in the proposed purchase. In contrast, the local group of investors had a better grasp of the financing problems, but knew little of the routine operation and business of LB. It was clear that the two groups had to cooperate in seeking to purchase the company; each was too weak to act alone.

Ladd and others saw an opportunity developing in which these groups could be joined in the attempt to purchase LB from Sperry.

The Sperry announcement forced people to rapid decisions and commitment to some action. Though the two groups had sought exclusive control for themselves, a rapid merger was required in order to present a quick response to Sperry, especially since the Sperry announcement did not include provisions for the sale of LB as an operating concern.

Eight days after the announcement, on Tuesday, April 6, 1976, the *Evening Telegram* and the *Observer Dispatch* carried headlines announcing the formation of the Mohawk Valley Community Corporation "to save the Library Bureau," and noted the backing of the LB union locals. Although the corporate charter papers were filed that day, the Mohawk Valley Community Corporation did not gain legal status as a corporation until April 15th. However, in announcing the filing of the corporate charter on April 6, the local press also publicized the MVCC's request to Sperry to delay the planned closing of the LB, and to come to terms over possible purchase offers that might be made.

The formation of the Mohawk Valley Community Corporation and its exposure in the press was only partially the product of motives based on saving the community; it was also the result of heated bargaining between the two groups. Rifenburgh was named chairman of the fledgling corporation, which was staffed by representatives of investment, LB management, and community interests.

The merger of competing groups into the new corporation was produced through the mediating role of John Ladd, director of MVEDD. In a series of dramatic meetings, Ladd forced the two groups to come to terms with each other and to recognize their common interests. The management group had been holding meetings with its own lawyer to determine the best course of action open to it. Similarly, the investors' group was dusting off its 1975 financing plan. On the Saturday three days following Sperry's announcement, the management group meeting in Utica was attended by Ladd who had convinced the investors group to attend as well. When Ladd had the members of both groups present together, he convinced them by force of argument to join forces.

It appeared that significant progress was achieved when Sperry announced on April 8th its agreement in principle to sell the LB division as an operating concern, and thus to postpone the closing and to negotiate. However, Sperry reportedly intended to proceed with its announced plans to turn away further orders for LB products, and to dissolve the 55-member LB marketing force. This, in the words of one observer, would have "reduced (the purchaser's) potency as a corporation to zero," as the new owners of the LB would come into control without any backlog of orders for equipment and without the marketing team required to obtain new business. Such a policy would make it difficult for the potential buyer to develop investors' confidence and financial backing, as the LB would have continuing operating expenses under new management without a guarantee of future income to meet them. Furthermore, Sperry made it clear that it would delay its original plans to begin phasing out the LB only if a purchase agreement could be reached in a matter of weeks.

Some observers questioned whether Sperry's offer was made in good faith. The offer was interpreted as an appeasement of public opinion which had been aroused against the corporation for the recent LB announcement and the Univac closedown in Utica the preceding year. The offer was also criticized because it held out little cause for investor confidence in a Library Bureau under new management. But in its own immediate interest Sperry could not hold out the promise of indefinitely delaying its decision, given that it had determined that the shutdown was required; to keep the sales force occupied would have meant increasing orders. Even if orders had been limited to short-run production activities, such action would have meant a delay in Sperry's ultimate objective. In addition, Sperry's earlier experience with local purchase attempts promised anything but local ability to conclude a sale. However, those observers who were involved from the community's side have interpreted Sperry's conditional agreement to negotiate and its ensuing actions as a form of obstructionism. Short deadlines and demands for down payments suggested that Sperry wanted to appear to negotiate while ensuring the failure of the local group.[1]

The MVCC was without capital or operating funds, but proposed to make an offer to Sperry for the purchase of LB. Another meeting was called, with 100 or so concerned community leaders invited, to lay out the plans of the corporation and to ask for donations. The chairman of the Herkimer County legislature, the mayor of Herkimer, investors, LB union and management leaders, and numerous citizens, including LB employees and their families, were present.

In the interim, the combined investment group developed a target financial plan from the plans drawn up in 1975. They proposed to raise capital in equity and loans through a loan of $2 million from the Economic Development Administration, channeled through the MVEDD, another $2 million in mortgage loans from area banks, and $1.8 million raised by selling common stock in the MVCC to willing investors. Before the EDA or the banks could be approached, it would have to be shown that there was interest in such MVCC common stock. The issuance of common stock would require a prospectus, or offering to the public, which in turn required a cash outlay to cover printing, mailing, and other costs. People would be needed to staff the stock subscription drive.

These problems were presented to the assembled community meeting, and the response was very positive. Numerous individual citizens, among them many LB employees and their relatives, pledged their time to support the subscription drive. A Concerned Citizens' Committee was formed to raise a targeted $15,000 to cover the expenses of the drive. Within three weeks, the committee had raised $16,000, $11,000 of which arrived within 24 hours of the committee's formation. These donations came from local

---

1. It is interesting to consider whether such perceptions served the cause of the community or not. If the community group required a closing of ranks to succeed, and it appears that this was the case, then perceptions of hostile intentions on Sperry's part may have forged public (and investor) opinion against a common enemy. However, it can be argued that such hostile perceptions may have slowed negotiations in the long run, as a result of the mutual suspicions they aroused.

merchants and private citizens, and the community meeting at Herkimer Community College became a rallying point in the community effort.

About the same time, Sperry announced its conditional willingness to sell the plant, and negotiations over a final selling price were taking place between Sperry representatives and MVCC at Sperry headquarters. A prospectus offering common stock in the MVCC was under preparation, and by the first week in May, 1976, the EDA had conditionally approved the proposed $2 million loan. The condition, however, was the raising of $2,000,000 in local equity capital through MVCC common stock purchases.

Work on the EDA loan application had been supervised by Ladd and others, but much of the actual work was carried out by a retired director of the MVEDD who agreed to assemble the material and write the application. He "shut himself in a basement" of the MVEDD offices for two weeks, and directed a small staff in researching the information required by the application. His efforts added to the local mythology building around the community's attempt to save the Library Bureau. Financial information for a feasibility study was easily available because LB management and Rifenburgh's investment group had already gathered the necessary details in their previous attempts to purchase the LB plant. Similarly, an EEOC compliance plan was easily available because Sperry had ordered one written for LB, and this was appropriated for the application. Help was also provided by the Technical Assistance Center at the State University of New York at Plattsburgh. This center was funded by the EDA and existed to aid economic development organizations like the MVEDD in northern New York. The two-inch thick final application, assembled in only two weeks, was itself a somewhat heroic effort in comparison to the norm in creating such documents.

During this same period the MVCC was negotiating with local commercial banks to obtain the third proposed block of capital. Ladd, in reviewing this period, recalls that it was difficult to convince the banks and commercial investors of the potential for MVCC's success. Ladd, the management group, and the investor's group were known to the local banks, as they had been approached by the former during the unsuccessful 1972-1975 purchase attempts. This kind of skepticism was shared by the EDA and the banks alike; in Ladd's words,

> It got to be the same way with the banks. So when we finally got this thing together, we really had to do some serious convincing. Not that these people were angry at us, but they had heard the same story so many times, and of so many innovative ways to do this thing which had never come to pass, that we had now to go in and really pound on their heads and say really this time it is going to work.

Up to this point, the effort had proceeded smoothly. However, on Monday, May 17th, in the words of one observer, "suddenly Sperry made waves." Sperry announced in Philadelphia that it would require MVCC to produce a $250,000 down payment, one which would not be refundable even in the event that the proposed sale did not succeed. In addition to a reluctance to abandon its original policy to close down LB and separately liquidate its assets, Sperry now believed that the cost of protracted negotiations and the uncertain promise that MVCC could raise the required equity made it mandatory to force the issue. Furthermore, Sperry refused to meet the MVCC negotiating demand that the LB marketing force be kept intact and the value of LB's assets in inventories and backorders be maintained while MVCC attempted to meet the financial and legal contingencies required by the EDA, the banks and those involved in preparing the stock prospectus. Negotiations broke off immediately when MVCC representatives perceived that Sperry had reconsidered its original agreements.

When word of Sperry's negotiating stance reached Ladd, Rifenburgh, and others, they mobilized every means available to them to bring pressure to bear on Sperry. They contacted Herkimer's mayor, the chairman of the county legislature, Representative Mitchell, Commissioner Dyson of the New York

State Commerce Bureau, congressional candidate Anita Maxwell, Senators Jacob Javits and James Buckley, and New York Governor Hugh Carey. Individually and collectively, these individuals contacted Sperry's chairman of the board, Paul Layette, and other Sperry representatives. Layette insisted that Sperry would have to see tangible evidence backing MVCC's good faith verbal statements. In turn, MVCC representatives argued that $250,000 simply wasn't available to the corporation, especially when they were forced to acknowledge to potential investors that the value and marketing potential of the LB could be drastically altered in the midst of the negotiations.

Representative Mitchell recalled the other plant closings Sperry Rand was undertaking in New York State and pointed to the poor publicity Sperry would receive if another plant were to close in the face of such obvious public enthusiasm for the survival of LB. Congressional candidate Maxwell, who was campaigning against Mitchell, had supporters in the National Farmers' Organization. She pointed out that her potential constituency in Herkimer was heavily represented by farmers, for whom the payments received from logs delivered to the LB sawmill were an important source of income. She threatened that if Sperry continued to obstruct the negotiations for the sale of LB, then she would attempt to organize a national boycott, through the farmers' organization, of Sperry's farm products line.

During the lapse in negotiations, while Sperry was being privately pressured, certain changes occurred in the makeup of the MVCC's board, which suggested a "tightening in the ranks." Early in May, the county legislature's chairman resigned from the board of directors of MVCC. When this was announced in the May 6th Utica *Observer Dispatch,* the item stated that he had resigned "not because of dissatisfaction, but because he felt that a conflict of interest might develop because of his chairmanship of the county legislature." In addition, Richard Karpen, who was to have been president and chief operating officer of the new corporation, also resigned his position on the board and took another executive position outside the community. Although the *Evening Telegram* reported Karpen's promise that he would be available to assist the new corporation during its formation, the changes appear to have improved the public image of the MVCC and may have represented some tacit compromise between the original competing groups.

On the 28th of May, negotiations were reopened between the MVCC and Sperry. All the pressure brought to bear on the company and its executives did not result in Sperry's withdrawing its demand for a down payment, although the lesser figure of $200,000 was agreed upon. However, Sperry did agree to refrain from breaking up the sales force and promised to keep inventories and back orders from dwindling. With this substantial concession in hand, MVCC executives set out to raise the down payment. As a first step, they called a meeting of LB employees on the evening of June 2 to discuss ways of raising the money.

They explained the situation to LB employees in terms of immediate capital requirements. Short term interest bearing notes would be exchanged for loans to the MVCC. These notes could be converted at a later time into stock purchase options at one-half the market price for MVCC shares when the shares came to the market. The employee response was overwhelming, and $193,000 was raised from the loans of more than 200 LB employees within two days. The only security they received for these loans were the promissory notes. Each employee investor took a substantial risk since the money was not refundable if the negotiations between Sperry and the MVCC ultimately failed. However, this money indicates that the employees were committed to supporting the purchase.

The LB's two unions, locals of the IUE representing clerical and blue-collar production employees, were indispensable in the drive to raise the down payment. Karl Vogel, the employee with the longest tenure in the plant (40 years' service), was president of the production workers' local. Earl Phillips with 10 years' service was president of the clerical workers' local. Vogel had attended meetings in the period 1972-1974 when management was discussing an attempt to buy the LB plant from Sperry and knew of the threatened closedown, but the matter had never before gone beyond the discussion stage.

When the actual announcement of the closing came, the union representatives and the employees were shocked and frightened. Management intentions to purchase the LB first caused confusion within the union and considerable indecision. Ladd planned to address a meeting of union members and non-union employees soon after the Sperry announcement and was dismayed to learn that the union officials had not invited union members. He contacted the union international and sought to calm and persuade; union cooperation was essential. The union, however, was unsure of its future role under employee ownership. Philips argued that representation and negotiation of pay, seniority, and benefits would still require the union. Some coaxing of the international was required before full participation of the locals occurred.

The union skepticism is understandable given the adversary nature of its relationship with management and the efforts of an unknown group of investors to buy the plant. Members of the MVCC board made it plain that continuance of the union was not in question, but the continuance of LB was—unless the union, as representatives of employees, would throw its weight behind the effort. The MVCC board of directors was so convinced of the importance of securing the union's support for the campaign and of assuring the union a sense of belonging that two seats on the board of directors were offered to the union. These were not accepted because board membership was not envisioned under union rules, and the international level of the union feared the creation of a conflict of interest. Even so, the union's role in plans to purchase the LB seemed a complicated question. The union was not permitted to purchase stock as a union, because it could not use its dues or other funds for this purpose.

Vogel has remarked that the call to raise the down payment did not seem problematic since the crisis overshadowed older relations between management and the union. The union could not spend its own funds, but it could provide direction and encouragement to its members:

> This was kind of a spot to be put on, but I said, "if we don't (raise the down payment) we're sunk; we're losing

our jobs and the area is going to suffer. Just give me a few hours and I'll get the ball rolling.'' So I immediately went right through the plant and got everyone enthused and in two days we came up with $193,000.

Sperry had specified a 45-day time limit during which its offer, to negotiate and sell, would remain open. Strangely, Sperry was evidently not prepared for such a speedy response with the down payment. When MVCC representatives tried to deliver the check for $193,000 they could not find anyone to accept it, and the transfer did not occur for another 10 days. The 45-day period was closing rapidly, and acceptance of the down payment put Sperry in the difficult position of holding $193,000 in nonrefundable community money while pressing for its deadline to be met. Eventually the 45-day period was extended by another 45 days.

The offering prospectus was almost complete when it was realized that Securities and Exchange Commission (SEC) regulations pertaining to successor corporations were an obstacle. Successor corporations, like the MVCC, seeking to purchase companies through a stock offering, are required by the SEC to provide certified financial documentation covering the previous three years of business. Since the major proportion of the MVCC's assets would be held in the LB, the regulations meant that MVCC would have to publish financial information on the LB which Sperry itself was unwilling to provide. Though MVCC's own accounting firm believed that the LB's operating statements were adequately monitored and trustworthy (members of the MVCC including Robert May had supervised the LB's operating budgets in their capacity as LB executives), the SEC required Sperry's independent certification of the information. Sperry was unwilling to make such representations because it feared contingent liability suits if the LB did not succeed under new management. As a result, MVCC found itself unable to put forth an offering document to the public. The promised EDA and bank loans, as well as the $193,000 raised by employees, were in jeopardy.

A solution to the problem was found when it was suggested that the MVCC contact the New York State Attorney General's office about the possibility of an intra-state offering. Unlike the federal government, the State Attorney General was authorized to waive certain requirements in a public stock offering. The New York State Department of Law agreed to assist MVCC in the registration of its offering document and accepted the operating statements. The only restriction that MVCC would suffer was the stock could not be bought or sold outside the state for a period of one year. The intra-state prospectus, filed April 15th, became effective July 1st, 1976, and under the deadlines set by Sperry, MVCC had until August 16th to raise the $1.8 million required before the commercial bank and EDA loans could be executed.

All of the MVCC's efforts were now turned to promoting the sale of its own stock. From the outset, it was policy that the new LB would be "wholly owned by the people of the valley, mostly by the employees." Restrictions were placed on the number of shares which could be owned by any one person (25,000 of the 1,000,000 shares issued). Such a policy, it was hoped, would ensure that the LB was managed in the interests of the community. But the problem of raising the capital in a short period was enormous. In Ladd's words,

> We started to sell stock and if you have never tried to sell
> $2 million worth of stock in 45 days in an area like ours,
> a depressed area, try it sometime. We brought in some
> experts who had been in sales . . . and they advised us
> that we should concentrate on the little guy in the street.
> What we call street financing.

To encourage the individual investor, local brokers were contacted and informed of the sale, and they agreed to advise potential customers. Furthermore, they agreed to sell the stock without receiving a commission. The local banks were approached by Rifenburgh, who urged that loans be made to individuals seeking to purchase stock, even if they presently held loans or had insufficient collateral. During the first day of the offering, the banks loaned $40,000 to private individuals for the purpose of investing in the stock. Similar pressure had been brought to bear on area banks when it was a question of raising the $200,000 down payment, and with the same success.

The campaign to bring the stock sale to the public's attention was directed at every person working or living within the Mohawk Valley. The campaign was staffed by volunteers, many of whom were the wives of senior LB employees. These volunteers alone were responsible for delivering over 13,000 copies of the 26-page prospectus. The local Chambers of Commerce distributed copies of the prospectus to their members. The Concerned Citizens for Library Bureau Committee sent out more than 6,000 letters explaining the campaign to educators in the five surrounding county school systems, and over 9,000 letters were mailed to librarians and affiliates in New York State.

Local television and radio media cooperated fully in the campaign. The mayor of Herkimer, who had a weekly talk show reporting community events, invited guests including MVCC board members, Lt. Governor Mary Ann Krupsack, and Representative Mitchell, to speak to the public. Individual investors bought stock by mail, by phone, or delivered their subscriptions on foot. In reviewing the campaign later, Ladd remarked that it appeared as though many of the smaller investors were not aware or did not understand the meaning of a stock sale, and thought they were donating money to support the LB.

Larger investors such as Utica Club Breweries, who saw how public opinion was swayed, took the opportunity of purchasing large amounts of stock and received publicity for it. Other potential commercial investors hoped that the MVCC could be induced to grant special concessions against the promise of purchasing the maximum 25,000 shares. Thus, MVCC was approached with proposals from insurance companies seeking exclusive contracts. These were turned down. One local entrepreneur sought to have the lease for his warehouse, which LB had used for several years, extended a full five years in exchange for stock purchases. When MVCC refused his offer, he refused to buy stock; and ultimately the MVCC moved out of the warehouse. By maintaining a policy of issuing no preferred shares, no concessions on the purchase of shares, and setting limits on the number of shares to be purchased by any one investor, MVCC tried to ensure that special interests within or outside the community were not able to dominate the company.

How was public support generated? Certainly, the presence of LB employees in the community, the generous coverage given to the campaign and the MVCC-Sperry negotiations and Sperry's negative image in the valley all helped. Nevertheless, the campaign was spearheaded by a carefully detailed plan to contact local elites and civic and commercial organizations. In the middle of June, shortly after Sperry had accepted the initial down payment, leaders of the MVCC campaign, including MVCC board members, local businessmen, and civic leaders met to decide on a strategy for the equity-raising drive. Minutes from the meeting show that the Drive Committee had tightly scheduled goals from review of the first draft of the prospectus to the inception of the fund-raising period. The minutes show that tactical objectives were established to draw support from all organized elements in the community.

The media: a) 'tombstone' announcements of the loss of LB to the community would appear in the press in Utica, Rome, Syracuse, Herkimer, Little Falls, Johnstown, Buffalo, and Albany; b) appointments would be scheduled for MVCC board members to appear on radio and TV talk shows.

Special programs: a) contacting New York State librarians by letter and through stock vendors; b) establishment of a $5,000 Club made of selected names from members of the community with individual Drive Committee members assigned to provide personal contact; c) a businessmen's kick-off luncheon to canvass the earliest contributors to the Concerned Citizen's Committee in May and the Business Assistance Committee in June to generate interest in the business community; d) an employees' meeting— after working hours—to encourage employees to locate six potential investors each; e) area educators; f) the unions; g) civic organizations, such as Lions, Kiwanis, Rotary; h) a Mayors' Conference encompassing all the Mohawk Valley; i) a special Doctors and Lawyers Drive; and j) general public drive.

The minutes of the Drive Committee also detailed target fund raising goals, and these are reproduced in full:

$5,000 Club	$ 200,000
Employees Drive	480,000
Herkimer Businessmen	150,000
Doctors and Lawyers Drive	100,000
Vendors Drive	300,000
Librarians Drive	200,000
BAC and Utica Businessmen	500,000
Frankfort Businessmen	50,000
Ilion Businessmen	100,000
Mohawk Businessmen	50,000
Little Falls Businessmen	100,000
Public Drive Businessmen	400,000
	$2,630,000

The campaign was similar to a United Way or Community Chest drive.

On June 30th, LB's 100th birthday, the public subscription prospectus became effective. The *Observer Dispatch* reported on July 1st that the purchase price of the LB stood at $5.1 million, and that the stock offering sought a maximum of $1.8 million or a minimum of $1.3 million in stock purchases.

Early on August 15th, the day before the deadline, accountants for MVCC found that it was still $370,000 short of its minimum goal. MVCC offices had remained open until 8 p.m. each night during the last week of the campaign, and would do so the 16th. The best estimates projected that between $200,000 and $300,000 would be raised, but the momentum of the subscription drive had been very unstable, increasing daily during the last week. During the same period, 123 TV and 500 radio spot advertisements had been used to attract the public. $100,000 in mail subscriptions were expected on the 16th and perhaps another $200,000 was expected in the form of walk-in purchases, but even with these generous estimates, the MVCC would still fall short of its goal by an estimated $70,000.

The MVCC still had unused resources at its disposal. In order to get the EDA to approve loan applications to localities, 5 percent of the total has to be obtained from local development agencies. The MVEDD, under John Ladd, apparently did not properly meet the local agency requirement, as it was formed under the regional jurisdiction of the EDA itself. The only organization which did fulfill the requirements was the Herkimer County Area Development Corporation (HCADC), under the direction of Henry Gaffey, who had supported Ladd in his earlier efforts on behalf of LB in 1972-1975. The HCADC had already agreed to meet the 5 percent minimum requirement. Now the MVCC turned again to the HCADC and asked if that organization would receive funds on behalf of LB if the Herkimer County legislature could be convinced to vote up to $150,000 to purchase LB stock.

The county legislature itself was not empowered to purchase stock, but MVCC made a request that the legislature's chairman arrange the stock purchase through a grant to the HCADC. In addition to these moves, MVCC had approached Sperry with a request for it to purchase up to $150,000, which at $2/share meant that 75,000 shares would be held by the previous owner. This request was made at the latest possible moment, and ran contrary to the MVCC's stock distribution policies. However, the request might also be seen in the light of the improved climate in the negotiations. If Sperry would buy, then the Herkimer County legislature would not have to vote any funds to the HCADC.

By noon on the 16th of August, Sperry had not responded to MVCC's request. Consequently, the legislature was alerted to be in session at 9 p.m. This would leave three hours in which to settle on a sum to put MVCC over its minimum requirement before the offering closed at midnight. Without the minimum $1.3 million, MVCC would have to return more than $1.1 million in subscriptions. Discussions between MVCC, the legislature, and Sperry hinged upon MVCC's ability to buy back $150,000 in shares in the future.

By 9 p.m., tensions eased somewhat when MVCC's shortfall was calculated at something under $100,000. Word arrived from

Sperry that it would back MVCC if necessary; the legislature was contacted and the eleventh-hour plan set aside. MVCC's future seemed guaranteed.

By midnight, however, MVCC had received $100,000 more than it needed in subscriptions, and Sperry was released from its last minute pledge. More than $500,000 had been raised in the final 24 hours. MVCC was very pleased with the support it had achieved; 3,500 stockholders from within the Mohawk Valley region and other points in the state would be the new owners of the LB when the sale was finalized September 28, 1976; over 30 percent of these were LB employees.

On August 27, 1976, Robert May, president of LB, informed the regional EDA office that the distribution of shareholding was as follows:

Share Amounts	No. of Subscribers
100	2,265
101 - 500	1,000
501 - 1,000	74
1,001 - 2,500	47
2,501 - 5,000	8
5,001 - 10,000	1
over 10,000 (11,000)	1

Approximately 3.5 percent of the shares were held by officers and directors. Thirty-five percent of the initial distribution was held by individuals working in the plant.

The detailed account of the effort to purchase the Library Bureau indicates the massive amounts of energy and coordination which are needed to complete a community-employee purchase. The importance of community leaders and organizational skills are shown repeatedly in the need to raise funds, negotiate between potentially conflicting groups and set up corporate structures. In communities where these skills are unavailable, community-employee purchases may not be a viable strategy to meet a plant shutdown threat. The combination of leadership skills available in Herkimer may have been an anomaly, but the existing supply of skills in other communities is unknown. Where leadership does not appear, purchase attempts are unlikely to succeed. The model of economic activity which relies upon a supply of entrepreneurial talent to explain innovation seems particularly appropriate with respect to the CEF strategy.

Subsequent Events

Although this study explicitly focuses upon the initial purchase decision, the long run performance of the firm is important. During the first year under community ownership (ending September 1977), MVCC showed a healthy profit of 34¢ per share and put aside $300,000 for the Employee Stock Ownership Plan. This represents $315,006 profit and $300,000 to the pension fund on sales of $11,192,905. During the year, the company purchased a steel bookstack manufacturing firm from a competitor and bought out two competing lines of library furniture. In the second year of operation, the company faced difficulties due to high start-up costs in the steel plant and difficulties in producing the new lines. An operating loss of 83¢ per share resulted in a decision to abandon production of the newly purchased lines. By the beginning of the third quarter of 1979, the profit picture had improved. The improvements were also a result of efforts to close a substantial number of accounts receivable. Detailed information is available in the Report to Stockholders.

REFERENCES

Bell, Daniel. *The Coming of Post Industrial Society: A Venture in Social Forecasting.* New York: Basic Books, 1976.

Crisafulli, Virgil. "Commerce and Industry" in *The History of Oneida County.* Published by Oneida County, 1977.

Department of Commerce. *Mohawk Valley Area Profile of Business and Industry: Business Fact Book Part I.* (1976 edition)

Herkimer County Budget: 1977. As adopted by the County Legislature, December 13, 1976.

Mohawk Valley Economic Development District: An Overview.

New York State Department of Labor. Manpower Planning Secretariat, *Economic Profile: Herkimer County, New York, Fall 1975.*

New York State Department of Labor. *Annual Planning Report, Fiscal Year 1976, Utica-Rome Labor Area.*

New York State Department of Labor. *Annual Planning Report, Fiscal Year 1977.*

New York State Department of Labor. *Labor Area Summary,* November 1977.

New York State Department of Labor, Division of Research and Statistics, Bureau of Labor Market Information. *Annual Planning Report, Fiscal Year 1978, Utica-Rome Labor Area.* Albany, June 1977.

New York State Department of Labor. *Labor Area Summary,* July 1978.

Sternlieb, George and J.W. Hughes. *Post-Industrial America: Metropolitan Decline and Inter-Regional Job Shifts.* New Brunswick, NJ: Center for Urban Policy Research, 1975.

Weinstein, Bernard L. and R.E. Firestine. *Regional Growth and Decline in the United States.* New York: Praeger, 1978.

PART II

COST-BENEFIT ANALYSIS: AN EVALUATION OF THE CEF STRATEGY

4
A Theoretical Framework

An evaluation of the CEF strategy is necessarily complex because of the variety and scope of issues which must be considered. For example, there is little basis to determine whether an evaluation should be aimed primarily at a long-run optimal solution for the economy as a whole or at a solution for a specific subsector or region. The mobility of capital may benefit the overall system, but create acute regional problems at the same time. Other issues raised by researchers include the allocation of social costs or externalities (Kapp, 1950); the apparent conflict between economic mobility and social integration (Olson, 1968; Warren, 1970; Crysdale, 1965; Haber, et al., 1963); and how to evaluate the many psychological (Manuso, 1977; Strange, 1977; Wilcock and Franke, 1963); sociopolitical (Brenner, 1976; Aiken, Ferman and Sheppard, 1968; Mick, 1975; Pellegrin and Coates, 1956); economic (Holen, 1976; Haber, et al., 1963); and psychophysiological (Selye, 1955; Kasl and Cobb, 1968) effects of unemployment at both individual and aggregate levels.

In addition to the economic, fiscal, sociological, and psychological issues themselves, each of them differs in the degree to which it may be quantified. Some aspects are measurable in either monetary or non-monetary terms, but others are only identifiable. The quantified benefits appear in the form of avoided costs as well as direct gains. Avoided costs are the losses which would have occurred in the community if the plant had closed. For

77

example, the difference between the wage and salary income obtained by MVCC employees and the income they would have obtained otherwise is an avoided cost. Other examples are the avoided drop in local tax payments, and an avoidance of an increase in local social service outlays. However, an increase in the amount of the firm's income which accrues locally is a direct gain. At the same time, the community has presumably gained by increasing its control over its economic base—a benefit which is unquantifiable.

Cost-Benefit Analysis

Cost-benefit analysis is a decision making tool which attempts to condense within some easily decipherable form (normally a ratio) the important advantages and disadvantages of any given project, and as a result, to aid an assessment of whether to proceed with such a project, as opposed to an alternative. The benefits and costs are normally identified according to their accrual over a specified period of time and, to enable the commensurate measurement necessary for a ratio, are presented in monetary terms.

While quantification of costs and benefits in monetary terms has been the norm, practitioners have recognized that many items relevant to an assessment of a project could not be monetized. A 1923 edition of *Engineering Economics* discusses such items as "irreducible data" which are also known as "judgment factors," "imponderables," and "intangibles" (Grant, Ireson and Leavenworth, 1976: 132). The classic passage from the Flood Control Act of 1936 which is cited as a basis of the cost-benefit approach recognizes both quantifiable and non-quantifiable criteria. It states that a project should be undertaken "if the benefits to whomsoever they may accrue are in excess of the estimated costs" *and* "if the lives and social security of people are otherwise adversely affected" (U.S. Code, 1940 ed.: 2694).

The critiques of cost-benefit analysis, both in theoretical terms and in practice, have been numerous and often well-founded (e.g., Somers and Wood, 1969). Prest and Turvey (1965) divided the limitations of cost-benefit analysis (concentrating on the usually more problematic benefits side) into four categories:

(1) *enumeration,* i.e., merely identifying fully the diverse benefits and beneficiaries can be very difficult, particularly with respect to the central question of whose viewpoint is to be used and the secondary problem of avoidance of the double counting of benefits;

(2) *evaluation,* i.e., "the vast jungle . . . of the measurability of utility" (Prest and Turvey, 1965: 729) is an issue which includes the problems of allowing for market imperfections and externalities even when market prices are available as benefit measures, questions of accounting versus opportunity costs, and valuation of collective goods;

(3) *choice of an appropriate discount rate,* the manifold problems of which can be summarized into the statement that "The ideal solutions . . . require knowledge of . . . yet unknown answers" (Prest and Turvey, 1965: 729); and

(4) *allowing (systematically) for uncertainty.* Interest rates and inflation may change, making cost and benefit estimates inaccurate.

It is also necessary to recognize that cost-benefit analysis is only a technique based upon a particular framework of constraints and considerations (budgetary, physical, legal, administrative) which have generally been decided upon in advance. It has rationality, but it is a limited rationality, based upon specific assumptions which are often arbitrary.

A further critique is that cost-benefit analysis tends to ignore the *distributional* aspect of projects. The technique concentrates upon whether the present value of benefits exceeds the present value of costs over some time period. It pays little or no attention to the persons or groups who accrue the benefits and incur the costs. Mishan points out that the use of cost-benefit criteria only "implies a concept of social betterment that amounts to a *potential* Pareto improvement" (1976: XII, his emphasis). For example, in this evaluation, the matter of main concern is to be whether, for the whole local community area of Herkimer, the benefits outweigh the costs; this ignores equity or other considerations regarding the specific persons within the community who appropriate the benefits.

The most trenchant criticism, however, is also the most general: that such analysis is simply unrealistic. Factors are chosen and quantified, and benefit-cost ratios obtained, without sufficient theoretical justification and without necessary sociopolitical and historical background. Cost-benefit analysis too often appears arbitrary. It is arbitrary in the sense of being the result of a particular paradigm. The evaluation obtained by a certain paradigm may have little basis for acceptance by those who have different preconceptions or who value different constraints.

There are several mechanisms which may be used to diminish some of these faults. The values of critical, but problematic, factors can be varied within the whole range of relevant possibilities. Such a sensitivity analysis permits an assessment of the manner in which uncertain factors in the analysis may change the overall evaluation. The analysis may be produced from the viewpoints of specific parties who are affected and provide insight into distributional aspects of the program under review. Benefits (and costs) may be explicitly weighted in the analysis according to equity considerations. For example, in the evaluation of community development corporations, Harvey Garn has suggested a scheme of "community welfare weights" (1975: 573-4). Also, practitioners of cost-benefit analysis are usually careful to stress that the results should be seen as only one of several inputs into a decision making process.

Despite its shortcomings, cost-benefit analysis provides an excellent framework for critical analysis and understanding of economic and social program options. It forces an enumeration of relevant decision factors and focuses attention upon comparisons among alternative actions at a given point in time. Future benefits and costs are considered in terms of their perceived values at the time a decision is to be made. The result of such an analysis is easily understood, and is intuitively appealing. These analyses may assist in bringing evidence into political decisions and avoiding the "pork barrel" approach which has characterized some federal government economic development programs (Kovarik and Devolites, 1977).

Level of Analysis

Most cost-benefit analyses are taken from the societal viewpoint. The object is an evaluation from the perspective of the entire social system, but the ideal is seldom reached because even the most significant social and economic ramifications of specific programs are difficult to trace throughout the society. The concern here is with community strategy in the face of plant shutdowns and an evaluation of the rationality of CEFs for the community first, and only afterwards does the societal level become the focus. This regional viewpoint means that the costs and benefits will appear radically different from those of a societal analysis. In fact, the benefits side for the community will include some items which a macro level analysis must view as costs. At the same time, moving the analysis to the community level permits precise examination of impacts and facilitates the illustration of the cost-benefit methodology, both in identifying relevant factors and measuring them.

This analysis also departs from common practice because of its multidisciplinary nature. Economic perspectives provide bases for calculating monetary costs and benefits involving wages, taxes, discount rates, etc., but psychology adds examination of the mental and physical health implications of job loss (Selye, 1955; Cobb, 1974). The sociologist's perspective on community elite networks (Laumann and Pappi, 1976) and the organizational structure of communities also suggests non-monetary considerations. The result is a broad analysis of the CEF strategy with the emphasis upon evaluation in the sense suggested by Weiss (1972: 29) that the importance of a program lies in its viability under particular environmental conditions. Do CEFs actually help create or maintain employment at a reasonable cost to a community and to the social and economic system?

Long and Short Term Perspectives on Saving Jobs

A fundamental issue confronting this evaluation is whether it is correct to attempt to save jobs at all. Regardless of short-run costs and benefits, society may be better off over a longer period by allowing capital to move unrestrained to uses which provide a higher financial return for private firms. Although economists regularly point to inefficiencies and market imperfections, the conventional presumption is that society's long-run welfare is increased by capital continually allocating itself through a decision making process in which private firms maximize their financial returns, and by labor resources moving from areas of insufficient demand to areas of sufficient or excess demand.

Schumpeter provides a classic formulation of this argument in his description of the "process of Creative Destruction," which is "the essential fact about capitalism" (1950: 83). He argues that

> First, since we are dealing with a process whose every element takes considerable time in revealing its true features and ultimate effects, there is no point in appraising the performance of that process *ex visu* of a given point of time; we must judge its performance over time, as it unfolds through decades or centuries. A system—any system, economic or other—that at every given point of time fully utilizes its possibilities to the best advantage may yet in the long-run be inferior to a system that does so at no given point of time, because the latter's failure to do so may be a condition for the level or speed of long-run performance. Second, since we are dealing with an organic process, analysis of what happens in any particular part of it—say, an individual concern or industry—may indeed clarify details of mechanism, but is inconclusive beyond that. Every piece of business strategy acquires its true significance only against the background of that process and within the situation created by it (1950: 83-84).

There is an analogy here to a population-ecology or systems model of economic change. The fitness of organisms for survival at a given point in time varies with environmental conditions. Capital is the basis upon which variation is built into the economic system and that system must maintain the "requisite variety" to meeting changing conditions. The short-run life or death of a particular unit contributes ultimately to the success of the overall system in the long run by ensuring the survival of units with the capability of adapting to environmental change.

Although costs are incurred by the society because of firms' activities, the unhindered performance of firms may result in a degree of long-run achievement that more than compensates for the short-run social costs. Presumably firms move, i.e., capital is reallocated, because changes in factor prices, changes in tastes, changes in technology, etc. alter the means through which capital obtains its highest monetary return. This relatively free movement of capital theoretically enables satisfaction of demand for goods and services and efficient production by adaptation to changed conditions. The market mechanisms active in the U.S. economy may constitute a "gale of . . . destruction" in Schumpeter's terms, but also "create" new, more efficient economic units (1950: 84). The implication is that the proposed shutdown of a plant is *prima facie* evidence that the jobs involved should *not* be saved.

These arguments are compelling, but must be challenged if only for their over-simplistic nature. Economic change also involves fiscal, organizational, psychological, and sociopolitical elements, each possessing both cost and benefit aspects. The Schumpeter model does not explicitly deal with the long term fitness of society on these topics. Neither is there a clear mandate giving long-run fitness a primary consideration over any short-run cost.

A pertinent example is provided by current capital reallocations to the South because of higher energy costs in the North. The capital flow presumably enables lower cost products for society than would otherwise be the case, but the reallocation also means that a society's long term investment in infrastructure in particular areas, designed partly for the support of industry, is underutilized. A dwindling number of members in a community remain to pay for transportation, education, and energy systems intended to service now-departed firms. This waste of resources is less than Pareto-optimal (Muller, 1975: 266). Further, individual workers may obtain higher wages by migrating to areas of growing demand for labor, but others have to accept lower rates and/or substantial unemployment. Migration may allow psychological growth through new experience, but it can also destroy a sense of community and of rootedness. The list of possible factors and their conceivable permutations is quite lengthy and the evaluation of such a list is both complex and controversial.

Conflicting Disciplines: Theoretical Bases for Analysis

The issues of time perspective and the non-economic effects of capital movement provide a basis for conflicting paradigms for analysis. By creating stereotypes of the economists' and sociologists' viewpoints, the conflict is not only made clear, but a basis for theoretical synthesis also becomes apparent.

Explicit recognition of the sociological-economic conflict has come from economist Mancur Olson (1968). Economists and sociologists carry ideal models of the functioning of society which, in several dimensions, are fundamentally incompatible. The economist's polar ideal focuses upon obtaining the optimal allocation of resources through mobility (of capital and labor) and innovation. Some sociological views (drawn largely from Parsons) value the maximization of social stability, institutional integration and avoidance of individual alienation. Olson argues:

> The economic and sociological ideals described are not only different, but polar opposites: if either one were attained, the society would be a nightmare in terms of the other. . . . The economic ideal required that there be an optimal allocation of resources at any moment in time and rapid innovation over time. An optimal alloca- tion of resources requires that a series of marginal con- ditions be satisfied throughout the society; the marginal rates of substitution of any two factors of production must be proportional to the ratio of their prices and the

same in all employments, and so on. But if there is rapid growth, the demands for different goods, the methods of production, the location of production, and the marginal products of particular factors of production will change incessantly. A Pareto-optimal allocation of resources will therefore require constant reallocations of resources. This will mean that factors of production, including labor, must frequently move from firm to firm, industry to industry, and place to place. Since methods of production are rapidly changing, the same combinations of labor and other resources won't be needed very long; new groupings of workers are needed as the economy changes. . . . Both social and geographical mobility are at a maximum in the economically "ideal" society, and there can be few, if any, stable group relations, apart from those in a nuclear family in which only one member is in the labor force. There can be no group loyalties or organizational constraints that limit individual mobility in response to changing incentives. There can be no organizations or other mechanisms that give those whose legitimate expectations are frustrated by the pattern of change the power to defend their interests, for this will (except where normally infeasible "lump sum" transfers can be arranged) pervert the pattern of incentives needed to bring about the resource reallocation which is entailed by the economic ideal. No group with a role in the productive process can restrict mobility by regulating entry, given privilege for seniority, or "featherbedding" (1968: 114-115).

The economists' and sociologists' paradigms tend to see different factors when they evaluate economic change or tend to value the same factors differently. When the elements of both perspectives are used at once, there is usually a perceived trade-off between the achievement of the values of each. Economic benefits, such as increased goods and services, lowest cost production, growth, and innovation appear to be negatively related to the ability to achieve benefits such as social stability, integration, rootedness, and avoidance of stress. The trade-off is produced by changes which require new combinations of inputs to production. Haber et al. (1963) viewed these changes which often produced plant shutdowns as the "impact of technological change" and decomposed them into (1) automation; (2) changes in machinery; (3) shifts in product demand; (4) mergers and consolidations; (5) changes in plant locational advantages; and (6) scientific management or time and motion study results.

In addition, there is a trade-off between long-run benefits of technological change, such as productivity increases, faster economic growth, more jobs, and higher employee benefits, and the serious short-run adverse effects on individual workers and sub-sectors of the economy.

Because of the overall long-run efficiency of market-determined decisions, this trade-off is such that society's welfare is increased by trying to resolve the short-run conflicts through facilitating the adjustment of individual workers to the necessary and eventually beneficial change.

As a result, the general approach of economic analysts is the one described in Wilcock and Franke's (1963) study of the closing at an Armour meat packing plant. The short-run social and economic costs are handled by retraining workers, relocation assistance, labor market information and unemployment insurance (Shultz and Webster, 1966).

Sociologists also recognize the trade-off but view such economic disruption with dismay because the strain placed on social relations produces alienation and disintegration. Economic dominance over social relations is a reminder that workers are basically treated as instruments of production and several neo-Marxist writers argue that this subjugation of the worker prevents individuals from achieving their human capacities (Meszaros, 1972; Lefebvre, 1972). Economic mobility is thought to result in the isolation of individuals and families. It destroys emotional contacts and positive attachments which promote a sense of belonging (Recard, 1975). Economists have tended to downplay these social costs because business decisions usually ignore them as well.

Evidence for the Trade-off

Roland Warren (1970) argued for a normative model in which society placed a value on the integrity of communities as a basic component of social structure. Communities must have autonomy regarding their economic fate, viability in the sense of a capacity to address problems from the community level, and wide distribution of decision making power among citizens. Community integration and stability is thought to derive from the power of self-maintenance rather than dependence upon outside control.

Empirical work reinforces this theoretical position. Strange (1977) studied a plant closing in a company town in Southern Appalachia and came to the conclusion that

> the plant closing in Saltville stripped that community of what had been its primary mechanism of social integration . . . it seemed to us that with its closing, Saltville lost not only its economic base and primary symbol of purpose and continuity, but behaviorally, the set of relationships which, beyond home and church, had traditionally related those men to each other and to the broader community. In other words, what seemed lost here was not only a job in a narrower sense, but a time-honored interaction network (Strange, 1977: 31).

A detailed study by Slote (1969) of the shutdown of a plant in Detroit found that the loss of the familial atmosphere in the plant plus other corollaries of job displacement were apparently related to negative psychological and psychophysiological effects. Subsequent effects found included alcoholism, hypertension, heart attacks, and ulcers. Several men died during the closing, including two suicides.

Crysdale, in his study of the social effects of plant relocation states that:

> this study shows that there appears to be a serious contradiction between the flexibility and mobility

required in rapidly changing industrial society and active participation in social and democratic processes (1965: 11).

Other researchers have found a relationship between job displacement and political alienation (Aiken, Ferman and Sheppard, 1968), and Long (1959) claimed that increases in absentee controlled business removed the business elite from real community participation, creating a vacuum of community leadership and domination by corporation interests.

Several studies have made the trade-off between economic and social welfare explicit. Mick analyzed shutdowns in the Connecticut rubber and plastics industry concluding that "shutdown costs, shutdown frequencies, and lack of shutdown protection suggests personal hardship is incurred whenever a plant closes its doors" and that "at some point, the social and personal costs of shutdowns will have to be weighed against economic costs" (1975: 208).

Kapp's book on social costs discusses the real or apparent conflict between rapid industrial change (and presumably growth) and the majority of people's preference to maintain the status quo and avoid instability (1950: 19). Lui's statistical analysis of the quality of life in the United States notes that "growth, it is charged, distorts national priorities, worsens the distribution of income, and irreparably damages the social and natural environments in which we all live" (1976: 37).

A United Steelworkers' union official, testifying in favor of proposed Ohio legislation which would, amongst other things, require companies which close plants to compensate the community affected with a payment equal to 10 percent of its dislocated employees' yearly gross wages, complained bitterly of communities being treated like "throw away containers."[1]

Labor economics studies also tend to reinforce the idea of economic gains accruing in the face of social losses. Despite economic gains to workers who relocate after a shutdown, a large

---

1. Frank Valenta, Testimony before the Committee on Ways and Means, Ohio State Senate, Columbus, Ohio, February 14, 1968.

majority are unlikely to move (Haber et al., 1963; Holen, 1976). Smith and Fowler (1964) obtained interviews with 145 workers out of 1,100 affected by a Ford plant closure in Buffalo, New York, and found that, despite the strong incentives of adverse labor market conditions in Buffalo, likelihood of lower monetary income, and guaranteed jobs in a new location (Lorain, Ohio), only 20 percent of their sample had taken the transfer offer about three months after the closure. They concluded that the high degree of immobility, which was seemingly irrational from an economic point of view, was largely a result of:

(1) a value system, as expressed in a life pattern of stability, which made stability an end in itself and predetermined the non-immigration answer;

(2) social ties and identifications which were locally strong and concentrated rather than diffused over a larger area, and which were not attached to mobile occupational or ethnic groups;

(3) economic positions which were meaningfully part of the local community pattern rather than part of a regional or national one (p. 47).

These reasons point to many workers', especially older workers', belief that their overall welfare is maintained by immobility, and that a large reason for this is maintained benefits of the kind defined here as social. American society in aggregate is remarkably mobile, but most of the people affected by the shutdowns discussed here do not want to move and often will not.

Despite the apparent importance of social costs, there is no consensus on an appropriate measure of the quality of social life, but an evaluation such as this one must take a broader view which permits criticism of the position that mobility provides an optimal solution in plant closings. One possible criterion of evaluation is the ability of a solution to minimize the mobility required to reintegrate displaced workers.

Is the Trade-off Inevitable?

There are a number of specific issues regarding the long- and short-run nature of this trade-off between net economic gain and social loss, but the idea itself provokes intriguing questions. Is the trade-off inevitable, leaving society with little choice but the application of partial solutions which ease the burden of displacement but nevertheless produce social costs? Olson (1968) suggests the trade-off itself may always exist in theory, but that there are opportunities to avoid both economic and social loss. These opportunities occur when society's resources are managed so inefficiently that both social and economic benefits are available through change. There is still a trade-off, but there are net gains to both social and economic welfare.

Community-employee ownership might provide a mechanism to improve both social and economic performance in some cases. To do this, however, CEFs would have to affect the parameters which determine performance in such a way that output could be increased without offsetting social losses—a result which has not been possible under conventional strategies for dealing with plant closings. Improved performance might come about through increased employee commitment, job involvement and productivity as well as corrections of potential errors in capital allocation. The following discussion considers economic welfare in terms of labor and capital efficiency and social welfare in terms of community stability.

Economic Welfare

Labor Inputs

Leibenstein (1966) argued that simple reorganization of firms could produce greater efficiency. Studies by McNulty (1977) and Shelton (1967) support his contention, and objections by economists such as Stigler (1976) have focused upon Leibenstein's desire to revise microeconomic theory rather than disagreement with the idea that efficiency gains are available. CEFs may have particular advantages in achieving some of these efficiency gains because of the manner in which they alter the relationship between workers and the means of production.

Motivation theory and evidence on job redesign suggest that when the interests of organization participants are congruent, rewards are directly tied to performance, and when high levels of commitment are present in an organization, performance will be increased, other things being equal (Vroom, 1964; Lawler, 1977; U.S. Department of Health, Education and Welfare, 1973; Davis and Cherns, 1975). Becker (1960) and Fox (1971) have argued the importance of "stake" to the nature of commitment, and Salancik and Pfeffer state that:

> It has been repeatedly found that when individuals are committed to a situation, they tend to develop attitudes consistent with their commitment and their committing behavior (1978: 230).

The employees' shares in a CEF give them a greater stake than in conventional firms. This stake ties personal gain to organizational gain and may produce attitudes and behavior consistent with increased productivity.

Though empirical findings which directly address this issue are limited, there is some evidence from studies of employee owned firms. Employee owned plywood companies studied by Berman (1967) have higher productivity than comparable conventionally owned firms. The Internal Revenue Service actually questioned the high wages paid by these firms relative to others because the IRS thought it was a ploy to avoid corporate taxes. The plywood cooperatives were able to show in court that their members' productivity was far enough above plywood industry standards to justify higher wage rates.

A lathe manufacturing plant in South Bend, Indiana was bought from its conglomerate owner through an Employee Stock Ownership Plan (ESOP), using an Economic Development Administration loan channeled through the local community. Productivity among its 500 workers is reportedly up 25 percent (*Wall Street Journal*, August 16, 1976).

The most sophisticated study to date is reported by Michael Conte and Arnold Tannenbaum, of the University of Michigan's Survey Research Center, who recently published data from a survey of 98 employee owned firms in the United States (1978). Sixty-eight of the companies have employee ownership under an Employee Stock Ownership Plan (i.e., via a trust) and 30 have direct ownership. Almost half of the firms had sales of at least $25 million during the year previous to the survey. Employees as a whole own at least half of the equity in about 75 percent of the companies.

Of particular interest is the profitability data, obtained from 30 firms. Conte and Tannenbaum calculated the ratio of pretax profits to sales for each company and then divided the results by the 1976 ratio for each industry represented. The average adjusted[2] profit ratio for the 30 companies was 1:7; the unadjusted ratio being 1:5. The authors claim these results "indicate greater profitability among employee owned companies than comparable sized companies in their respective industries" (p. 25). Statistical significance is not achieved, however, as the sample is small and includes relatively large variance in profitability.

Regression analysis of employee ownership-related predictors of profitability found that, although a large amount of variance was explained by the predictors, only the percent equity owned by non-managerial employees had a statistically significant relationship. The results are given in Table 4-1.

The authors point out that the presence of negative associations with the other predictors does not imply (even if they were statistically significant) that such factors have a negative effect on profits except under the conditions of this regression analysis. In reality, these factors may be tied to percent equity held by workers, and it is only by statistically controlling the latter factor that the others are found to have the negative relationships. This point applies to four of the other predictors, as shown by the table of zero order correlates.

---

2. For five directly owned companies, the profit figures had to be adjusted because they distributed a portion of their "profit" as wages. The sum of average wage differentials between worker owners and nonowner workers was added to the formal profit figures in each of these companies.

Table 4-1
Regression Coefficients for the Predictors
of "Adjusted" and "Unadjusted" Profitability

Predictor	Adjusted	Unadjusted
ESOP (= 0) vs. direct ownership (= 1)	-.22	-.34
Percent employees participating in plan	-.30	-.31
Percent equity owned internally ...	-.31	-.19
Percent equity owned by workers ..	1.02*	.78
Worker representatives on board of directors	-.18	-.18
Employee stockholders vote	-.05	-.24
Multiple r.....................	.72	.47

Source: Conte and Tannenbaum, *Employee Ownership,* 1978, p. 25.

Note: The data necessary to calculate the adjusted profitability ratio was unavailable in five companies of the subset and five companies did not provide information concerning all of the predictors in this regression. The number of cases in the adjusted and unadjusted cells are therefore 20 and 25, respectively.

*p < .02

The analysis is particularly noteworthy because it supports the common sense idea that lower-level workers are only more productive when it is directly in their interests to be so. The other predictors, without the crucial factor of workers owning much of the equity, are characteristic attributes of employee participation schemes, and of situations where the managers, rather than the workers, are the major beneficiaries of the firm's activities (i.e., "percent owned internally" factor). The implication is that participation schemes without a substantial component of the benefits accruing to workers will not be much help in raising profits. Appraisals of participation plans by Brimm (1972, 1975) and Nord (1974, 1975) further support this contention. CEFs provide such a benefit for the worker owners and might be able to improve performance.

Table 4-2

Correlations Among Aspects of Employee Ownership and Profitability

Characteristics	Profit (adjusted) (N = 20)	Profit (unadjusted) (N = 25)	Stock plan vs. direct ownership (N = 75)	Percent employees participating (N = 75)	Percent of equity owned internally (N = 75)	Percent of equity owned by workers (N = 75)	Workers on board (N = 75)
ESOP (= 0) vs. direct ownership (= 1)	.48*	.27					
Percent employees participating	-.33	-.29	-.23*				
Percent of equity owned internally	-.02	-.06	-.10	.25*			
Percent of equity owned by workers	.60*	.31	.68*	.14	.34*		
Workers on board	.24	.08	.36*	.08	.04	.43*	
Employee stock-holders vote	.30	.18	.68*	.11	-.11	.47*	.22*

Source: Conte and Tannenbaum, *Employee Ownership,* 1978, p. 26.

*p $<$ .05

Conte and Tannenbaum were also concerned with managers' subjective appraisal of employee ownership. In general, managers in the 98 firms thought employee ownership had a positive effect on workers' attitudes, productivity, and firm profitability. They also report a detailed study of a firm which had recently adopted an employee ownership plan. Company records showed that grievances and waste had declined, and that productivity and profitability had risen in the period immediately after the introduction of the plan. The authors conclude:

> If employee ownership does have an effect on the economic performance of a company, as the data of this study tentatively suggest, the explanation may be found, at least partly, in the effect of ownership on the employees themselves (p. 28).

Further evidence is provided by a study comparing 12 Israeli manufacturing firms, half conventionally run by "management" and half "cooperatively" run by Kibbutzim (Melman, 1975). Six matched pairs of firms, including tool manufacturing, die casting, plastics, machine shop, and canning were compared on productivity of labor and capital, as well as profits per worker and costs of administration. Table 4-3 summarizes the comparisons by listing the better performing firm in each industry or both if equal performance was apparent.

Though the study examines only a small number of cases at a single point in time, the results at least suggest that "cooperatively administered industrial enterprises can be as efficient, or more efficient, than managerially controlled units" (Melman, 1975: 212), and an analysis of the capital assets of the firms supports organization structure rather than size as the explanation for the findings.

Two case studies by researchers in the New Systems of Work and Participation Program at Cornell University provide some additional insights. Long's (1978) study of a trucking company in Canada owned by most of its employees showed substantial improvement in organizational performance. Labor turnover declined 30 percent and damage claims by 60 percent in the first

Table 4-3
Summary Ranking of Managerial (M) versus Cooperative (C)
Enterprises by Criteria of Efficiency

Industry	Sales per man hour	Profit per worker	Profit/ capital	Sales/ assets	Administrators/ production workers
Tools	M	M	M	C-M	M
Instruments	M-C	M	M	C	C
Die casting	M-C	C	C	C	C-M
Plastics	C	C	C	C	C-M
Machine shop	C	C	C	C-M	M
Canning	M-C	C	C	M-C	C

two years of operation. Freight handler productivity improved by 5 percent, and a substantial profit was made compared to losses the previous five years. Long also found higher levels of worker integration, involvement, commitment, and satisfaction. Moreover, participation in plant decision making had not changed, permitting Long to attribute many of these improvements to the ownership change.

Similar improvement in the quality of upper and lower level employee input has been found in the study by Gurdon (1978). In this case, a small knitting mill owned by a medium-size corporation had performed well until it was sold to a much larger corporation, Cluett-Peabody, in 1968. By 1974, after some major management errors, sales volume had dropped about 70 percent, the mill suffered a loss of $11 million, and Cluett-Peabody decided to cut back the work force and eventually close the plant. Under the direction of the top manager, a group of the employees bought the firm in 1975. The company president, freed from the constraints and mistakes of Cluett-Peabody, made changes which have restored the mill's profitability. Regarding lower level employees, there have reportedly been significant cost savings in quality control, wastage, plant cleaning, and pilferage.

Analysis of labor productivity is particularly difficult to obtain, and direct evidence is not available on the MVCC case, though the firm has certainly been in an improved position since the ownership change. The exact cause of the improvement may only be inferred. The issue raised here, however, is that CEFs may benefit from their ownership structure in terms of labor productivity. If so, the CEF strategy in plant shutdowns would minimize the trade-off by improving economic outputs without incurring social loss.

Capital Inputs

The process of plant closure and loss of jobs is triggered by the functioning of the capital allocation market. The assumption that correct decisions are made in this market is questionable, and CEFs provide a possible mechanism to improve market performance by correcting several types of capital market failure. The assumption of proper functioning may be criticized on the grounds that (1) the allocation process does not make correct decisions even according to its own criteria, and (2) the allocation process itself is somehow incorrect.

Stephan Michelson (1977) develops these critiques in an analysis of four types of capital market failure. He begins by categorizing production costs conventionally as monetary or non-monetary and internal or external. The costs are classified according to their appearance in calculations regarding a firm's production process, and internal-external refers to the inclusion of a cost in the firm's accounting system. Most companies are concerned only with internal monetary costs. Michelson then defines the four types of market failures.

1. Market Failure 1 (MF1) occurs when the capital market fails to place capital where it makes a maximum internal monetary return through ignorance of the opportunity.

2. Market Failure 2 (MF2) occurs when the capital market does maximize internal monetary return, but by other criteria (the other costs of production) the capital allocation is "wrong."

3. Market Failure 3 (MF3) occurs when an actor in the capital market is aware of the opportunities to increase internal monetary return but is constrained from doing so.

4. Market Failure 4 (MF4) occurs when the capital, whether maximizing only internal monetary return or social return, given the resources available to it, fails to produce the return it would without additional cost through a change in some legal form such as ownership and control (1977: 11-12).

These analytic categories are not exclusive, and a situation may involve some or all of such failures. An evaluation of community-employee ownership is important to this analysis because suggestive evidence of all these types of failures can be seen in the case being studied. Can the circumstances in this case and the CEF form of ownership produce more efficient use of capital?

Market Failure 1

The situation where capital allocations are inefficient because of inadequate information regarding opportunities for their use is the most conventional form of failure. However, the *relative* efficacy of CEFs may be the *lowest* in regard to MF1. The argument is based on the idea that persons with local or specialized knowledge may see opportunities not heeded by the conventional capital allocation process dominated by large corporations. Although this advantage is presumably a facet of CEFs, it derives from being a *local* process rather than solely from being a community-employee ownership one. Conventional private, but local, ownership will presumably also have this advantage. Thus, as evaluations must properly consider *differences* between alternatives, the advantages of CEFs especially lie in correcting other types of failures. However, in the case considered here, the CEF strategy was the only one available to establish local ownership.

There are indications of MF1 in the MVCC case. The motivation behind Sperry Rand's decision to close down the Library Bureau is not entirely clear, but may have resulted partially from ignorance of the means by which their return on capital could be increased. The new management increased the firm's profitability and probability for its future prosperity by acting on their intimate knowledge of the library furniture industry and market. Their market position was strengthened by purchasing a competitor's product line. The new management saw that a new drying kiln would both aid their productivity and provide additional revenue (through selling dried lumber not used in the plant). Information was obtained on new markets, and the firm began selling overseas (Middle East) and promoting a new line of office furniture.

Lack of information and action may have operated on two levels. Sperry's top management was primarily involved in electronics, and may have been disinterested in a small library furniture factory in upstate New York, which was obtained as a by-product of a merger. The information on which the MVCC acted was available to Sperry; in fact, expansion to the Middle

East had been suggested earlier, but the top Sperry Rand leadership was not interested in seeking it out.

Ignorance of opportunities may also be associated with Sperry's use of the Library Bureau as a training ground for Sperry Rand management. According to reports of current firm managers, there was a continual procession of management personnel, none of whom stayed long enough to become fully knowledgeable of the business, or, who had little motivation to make substantial changes because they would not be there long enough to personally profit from them.

Market failures which occur because of lack of information on opportunities suggest that some plant closures might be avoided if the relevant decision makers were less ignorant about opportunities to increase returns. The evidence in the MVCC case exemplifies this form of failure in the sense that opportunities were ignored, but full information might not have altered Sperry's particular decision. Sperry may have obtained higher returns in the electronics industry than in the library furniture industry, even with a firm in the latter operating under the most ideal conditions. In this situation, the correct decision according to conventional firm-oriented criteria is to switch capital from a use such as the Library Bureau to a means of gaining higher returns. This type of market failure, though perhaps the one most likely to be exploited by CEFs in the near future, is least applicable to an evaluation of the differences between CEFs and more conventional approaches to job saving.

Market Failure 2

Market Failure 2 is more critical to an evaluation of CEFs because it argues that capital allocation based only on internal monetary criteria is "wrong" in the sense that it ignores the other costs of production which are generally termed "social" (Kapp, 1950) or "externalities." Assuming that these costs should be counted, CEFs are much less liable to MF2 errors. CEFs will take social costs into account because such factors affect the interests of the parties comprising the firm ownership.

The traditional (Schumpeterian) objection to use of social costs is that long-run firm performance, unhindered by social cost concerns, will make up for the costs imposed. Lack of evidence for both the traditional and social cost accounting viewpoints makes the issue highly debatable. A substantial body of literature has developed which argues that Schumpeter was incorrect and that better social accounting will show the crucial importance of social cost considerations.

The contemporary analysis of social costs is generally traced to Kapp, who defined these costs as "those harmful consequences and damages which third persons or the community sustain as a result of a productive process and for which private entrepreneurs are not easily held accountable" (1950: 14). While he recognized the short-run optimality of externalizing costs, he questioned the stability of such a system because those asked to pay the social costs were likely to oppose the productive process. Changes regarding pollution regulations, workers' compensation and unemployment insurance represent a recognition of these costs.

More precise social accounting criteria have been suggested by the American Institute of Certified Public Accountants in a book titled, *The Measurement of Corporate Social Performance* (1977). It suggests that firms begin to collect information on

(1) participation in community service and quality of life activities;
(2) plant location and relocation;
(3) direct employee-related effects (income, psychological, opportunities given, etc.);
(4) utilization of local businesses;
(5) impact on the physical environment;
(6) impact on sociopolitical infrastructure and cultural activities (1977: 162-3).

Since plants often relocate rather than simply close, the accountants suggest a procedure which "would show both the positive and negative effects on the two communities and the net consequence to society" (p. 160).

There has been a constant stream of research reports which argue for social audits, corporate responsibility and human resource accounting (e.g., Brummet, Pyle and Flamholtz, 1968; Chastain, 1973; Davis and Bromstrom, 1975; Edmunds, 1976). Firms are sometimes forced to provide some compensation for these costs, particularly when faced with public outcries and union contracts. Some states are beginning to require severance pay, but such factors are clearly subsidiary in the decision making process regarding plant closures.

For example, Whitman and Schmidt (1966) published a detailed study of the process by which General Foods Corporation closed down four older plants and consolidated their operations at a new location. The study is regularly cited as showing the ideal for corporate behavior in such situations (Management and Economic Research, Inc., 1978). The social cost concerns we have been discussing are dealt with in the chapter on public relations. Similarly, Sperry Rand appears to have seen the community effects of plant closing as being primarily a public relations problem.

This is not to suggest that the social sanctions implied in the concept of a public relations problem are not real. In fact, through the strong threat of political repercussions by political representatives, Sperry Rand was forced to take account of social costs and ultimately removed a major blockage to the MVCC purchase. However, during the same period as the Library Bureau purchase, Sperry Rand also decided to close a large Univac plant in nearby Utica. A major campaign, including pressure from the state senators, the governor, and local politicians (as well as substantial financial incentives) had no apparent effect on Sperry's decision. The plant was phased out in early 1977 with the direct loss of about 1,000 manufacturing sector jobs. The social costs imposed had no major role in the decision making process by which the capital needed to provide the jobs was reallocated.

In contrast, a CEF would have had to give more weight to the costs associated with social demands, at least to the extent those costs are imposed on the local community and the employees. The case for considering social costs is a strong one, and these factors have been included in the cost-benefit analysis. Differences between CEFs and alternative job saving methods regarding concern for social costs are important to the evaluation.

Market Failure 3

Michelson points out that the conventional capital allocation process sometimes fails to maximize returns, not because of an inability to identify opportunities or not wanting to act upon them, but because of legal, social, or size constraints. He notes that:

> Inability to put land packages together, inability to finance, or countervailing forces (environmental protection or costs imposed by a militant population, for example), sometimes block the placement of capital. The public power construction done by the Tennessee Valley Authority is an example of government action in the face of Market Failure 3. Redlining, another example, occurs when individual banks, fearing that other banks will not lend in an area, themselves refuse to risk investment. This might be considered a problem of scope, an inability to control the total flow of capital in an area or a "fallacy of composition." Each institution fears that other capital may not be forthcoming, and, to avoid risk, withdraws. Looking back, their action will have been justified, even though, overall, profitable opportunities actually did exist (1977: 4).

MF3 is appropriate in the MVCC case because one of the constraints which affected capital movement, and thus job availability, was size. Local private buyers individually had neither sufficient capital nor enough political support to make the Library Bureau purchase; a combined community effort was needed. The community, including the employees, together were a large enough group to supply the necessary risk money and equity. The combined entity was large enough both in the sense that the resources could be obtained, and in the sense that it could take the risk because the investment of any given individual was small. The community-wide effort attained a degree of legitimacy which made the vital political support and government financing easier to obtain. A conventional private organization or one with a narrow support base would not have obtained the widespread voluntary help which enabled the extraordinary "Save the LB" campaign or the general public's sympathy and interest.

The MVCC does appear to have overcome a market deficiency, partly based on size, and partly on its unique base of support. The local entrepreneurs who were aware of the returns to be obtained from the LB were too small in terms of financial resources to make the purchase. Organizations large enough to buy the Library Bureau were uninterested or unaware. The CEF filled the gap and saved the jobs.

Whether the size and flexibility of a CEF is always appropriate is problematic. This organizational form has some advantages where conventional organizations are constrained, but limited at other points. Small firms face the chronic problems of small business such as the inability to absorb miscalculations or take advantage of economies of scale. There are probably severe limitations on the total amount of capital which could be raised. Thus, buying a steel plant, such as Youngstown Sheet and Tube, is far more complex and the organizational form of the CEF may require adjustment.

At the same time, the CEF provides an option which was usually outside a community's range of solutions to job creation and maintenance. Similar locally based community development corporations have sometimes been able to overcome difficulties resulting from area racial composition. Involving local residents in business development has been successful in the Bedford-Stuyvesant Restoration and Development Corporation and the East Los Angeles Community Union.

Market Failure 4

This form of capital misallocation has the most intriguing economic and political implication. Michelson suggests that greater returns might be available if the form of ownership were changed. He asks "whether the return to the activity is the same when outsiders are owners" (1977: 10). In an argument consistent with the notion that local control will increase productivity, Michelson remarks that different rates of return may come to an enterprise under different owners. In this case:

> The capital market is correct to leave and the workers are correct to purchase. This is a potentially powerful argument. It says that by restructuring the ownership of a stock of physical capital, the capital can become more productive. . . . In terms of real resources, changing the form of ownership may get you something for nothing (p. 10).

This is precisely the argument advanced by other writers such as Louis Kelso (1958) who have advocated Employee Stock Ownership Plans, but it is also consistent with the idea that local ownership and control, with or without the workers may be more effective than absentee ownership.

Potential gains to worker controlled firms discussed earlier in this chapter must be weighed against potential difficulties, particularly when workers are first becoming involved in decisions. Worker owners may over-allocate current company income to consumption, risking investment capability. Collective decision making requires practice to avoid slow reaction time and excessive conflict, and workers may resist technological changes which threaten jobs, thus perpetuating obsolete technology.

Size and Technology

Discussions of organizational productivity inevitably mention the importance of firm size and the technology of production, but these variables have ambiguous effects or are inappropriate for a case study such as this one. Size contributes to technical efficiency through economies of scale (Bain, 1968), but the contribution may reach its maximum at a fairly small size (Stein, 1974). Most employee owned firms are fairly small and claim advantages in the psychological health of workers (Kornhauser, 1965; Kirsch and

Lengermann, 1972; Kohn, 1976), increased flexibility, and reduced administrative costs. At the same time, they suffer the disadvantages discussed earlier regarding capital and the ability to absorb adversity. The relevant issue for comparative study is whether the employee or employee-community form of ownership can be adapted to a large scale organization.

Technology presents a similar problem since it is largely determined by the type of output the organization wishes to produce and the capital invested. Most cooperatives have been in labor intensive industries, and the critical issue is whether the cooperative form itself can exist in capital intensive production or if the capital required has simply been too large for most of these organizations. There is no clear theoretical rationale for arguing that the size or technology in a plant threatened with closure will alter the production transformation curve. However, comparative studies focused upon these variables might show that size and technology constrain the ability to initiate a CEF. This case cannot adequately address the issues involved.

SOCIAL WELFARE

The positive benefits which accrue socially are more difficult to enumerate because most social indicators of the quality of life appear as avoided costs in this analysis. That is, economic welfare might increase, but social welfare remains constant by avoiding the stigma of unemployment, the increase in psychological stress, marital disputes, etc. Avoiding social costs is a benefit in itself compared to other shutdown cases, but such benefits are available from standard retraining, supplementary income, and relocation assistance. However, one critical benefit derives from the particular form which the establishment of a CEF takes.

The community sociologist argues for community viability in terms of local ability to cope with local problems. Communities should have the ability to determine their own economic fates to the greatest degree possible. Absentee control presumably decreases this ability and leaves communities in the hands of national or at least extra local actors. The ability to solve local problems is a function of local resources consisting of capital, knowledge, and the capacity to mobilize these resources. The last factor is most important as capital sitting in banks and mattresses or knowledge of how to obtain federal funds are of little use without the ability to draw on these resources and use them effectively. The use of resources requires a supply of human energy and the ability to coordinate effort. Without organizational skills and an organizational basis for action, little is accomplished.

Organizational capacity is a critical element in political conflict at all levels, from local decision making through interest group efforts to influence legislatures to revolutions. Influencing community decisions requires an organizational basis of power from which to mobilize population. Laumann and Pappi (1976) show the importance of elite-organizational connections in the German community they studied, and Crain, Katz, and Rosenthal (1968) provide evidence of the importance of organized interests in fluoridation controversies.

Current interest in a resource mobilization approach to social movements is more to the point. Organizations are required for "mobilizing supporters, neutralizing and/or transforming mass and elite publics into sympathizers, achieving change in targets" (McCarthy and Zald, 1977: 1217). Revolutions apparently result not only from high levels of discontent (which always exist), but also from the existence of organizations which may be used to mobilize population resources (Oberschall, 1973). The infrastructure of organizational relationships controls the ability of a social unit such as a community or political interest to act.

As a result, a community with few organizational units or a number of organizations controlled outside the community will lose the ability to act in its own behalf. Low levels of organizational capacity would make community action to save a threatened plant more difficult, but when the effort has been made, as in the establishment of a CEF, new relationships have been created and organizational capacity increased. Thus, the successful mobilization effort leaves the community in a better position to handle future crises in terms of knowledge, skills and the ability to mobilize resources. The creation of a CEF may produce an increase in social welfare without cost to the economic side.

CONCLUSION

The theoretical perspective proposed here suggests that the traditional unalterable trade-off between economic and social welfare bears reexamination and that CEFs may provide an opportunity to move the output of benefits to a higher product transformation curve. The discussion is still largely theoretical, but it provides one possible answer to Michelson's argument that community-based economic development requires a framework and language which permits communities to explain why the community should be the basis of economic activity. Local control through CEFs may result in: (1) better information regarding investment opportunities; (2) the consideration of social costs; (3) increased productivity; and (4) improved ability of the community to meet future crises.

At the same time, the traditional trade-off view has developed evidence supporting the notion that plant closings reflect correct market reactions to changes in taste, technology and production costs, and that in the long run, society is better off by leaving economic change to occur unencumbered. Even if market failures exist, correcting them could represent only minor, fine tuning of the capital market and scarcely merit attention. Social costs are handled by society and, given time, the social system adjusts.

Though the cost-benefit analysis addresses many of these questions, it is impossible for a single case study to resolve all of the points raised in the discussion. Such questions are only resolvable by society's expressions of preferences for economic and social goods through the political process and individual choices. What this cost-benefit analysis does is give an example of which factors can be considered, what methodology is appropriate for evaluating them, and what conclusions may be drawn regarding the specific events in the Mohawk Valley.

REFERENCES

Aiken, Michael, L.A. Ferman, and H.L. Sheppard. *Economic Failure, Alienation and Extremism.* Ann Arbor, MI: University of Michigan Press, 1968.

Bain, Trevor. *Defense Manpower and Contract Termination.* Tucson, AZ: University of Arizona, College of Business and Public Administration, Division of Economics and Business Research, 1968.

Becker, Howard. "Notes on the Concept of Commitment," *American Journal of Sociology,* 66, July 1960, pp. 32-40.

Berman, K.V. *Worker-Owned Plywood Companies: An Economic Analysis.* Pullman, WA: Washington State University Press, 1967.

Brenner, M. Harvey. "Estimating the Social Costs of National Economic Policy: Implications for Mental and Physical Health and Criminal Aggression," in *Anchoring the Goals of the Employment Act of 1946-30th Anniversary Review,* Vol. 1, paper No. 5, Washington: Government Printing Office, 1976.

Brimm, Ian M. "Analytical Perspectives in Organizational Behavior: A Study of an Organizational Innovation." D.B.A. dissertation, Harvard University, 1975.

Brimm, Ian M. "When is a Change Not a Change?" *Journal of Applied Behavioral Sciences,* 8, 1, 1972, pp. 102-107.

Brummet, R. Lee, W.C. Pyle, and E.G. Flamholtz. "Accounting for Human Resources," *Michigan Business Review,* 20, 2, March 1968, pp. 20-25.

Chastain, Clark A. "A New Role for Accountants: Accounting for Environmental Expenditures," *Business and Society,* 14, 1, Fall 1973, pp. 5-12.

Cobb, Sidney. "Physiologic Changes in Men Whose Jobs Were Abolished," *Journal of Psychosomatic Research,* 18, 1974, pp. 245-258.

Conte, Michael and Arnold S. Tannenbaum. *Employee Ownership.* Report to the Economic Development Administration. Ann Arbor, MI: Survey Research Center, 1978.

Crain, Robert L., Elihu Katz, and Donald B. Rosenthal. *The Politics of Community Conflict.* Indianapolis: Bobbs-Merrill, 1968.

Crysdale, Stewart. *Social Effects of a Factory Relocation.* Toronto, Ontario, Canada: Religion-Labor Council of Canada and the United Steelworkers of America, 1965.

Davis, Keith and R.L. Bromstrom. "Implementing the Social Audit in an Organization," *Business and Society,* 16, 1, Fall 1975, pp. 13-18.

Davis, Louis E. and A.B. Cherns. *The Quality of Working Life,* 2 vols. New York: The Free Press, 1975.

Edmunds, Stahrl W. "Social Responsibility, Neglects, and Reticulation," *Business and Society,* 16, 2, Spring 1976, pp. 21-28.

Effrat, Marcia P. "Approaches to Community: Conflicts and Complementarities," *Sociological Inquiry,* 43, 3-4, 1973, pp. 1-32.

Faux, Geoffrey. "Politics and Bureaucracy in Community Controlled Economic Development," in *Law and Contemporary Problems.* Duke University, School of Law, Spring 1971. Excerpted in Center for Community Economic Development's *Community Economics,* May 1971.

Fox, Alan. *The Sociology of Work in Industry.* London: Collier-Macmillan, Ltd., 1971.

Garn, Harvey A. *Program Evaluation and Policy Analysis of Community Development Corporations.* Washington: The Urban Institute, June 1975.

Government Operations, Hearings Before the Subcommittee. "Operations of the Community Sources Administration." Washington: Government Printing Office, 1977.

Grant, Eugene L., W.G. Ireson, and R.S. Leavenworth. *Principles of Engineering Economy.* New York: Ronald Press Company, 1976.

Gurdon, M.A. *The Structure of Ownership: Implications for Employee Influence in Organizational Design.* Unpublished Doctoral dissertation. New York State School of Industrial and Labor Relations, Cornell University, 1978.

Haber, William, L.A. Ferman, and J.R. Hudson. *The Impact of Technological Change.* Kalamazoo, MI: W.E. Upjohn Institute, September 1963.

Holen, Arlene. *Losses to Workers Displaced by Plant Closure or Layoff: A Survey of the Literature*. Arlington, VA: Center for Naval Analyses, November 1976.

Jacobson, Louis S. *Earning Losses of Workers Displaced from Manufacturing Industries*. Public Research Institute publication, No. PP 169, November 1969.

Kapp, K. William. *The Social Costs of Private Enterprise*. Cambridge, MA: Harvard University Press, 1950.

Kasl, Stanislav, Sidney Cobb, and G.W. Brooks. "Changes in Serus Uric Acid and Cholesterol Levels in Men Undergoing Job Loss," *Journal of American Medical Association,* CCVI, November 1968, pp. 1500-1507.

Kelso, Louis O. *The Capitalist Manifesto*. New York: Random House, 1958.

Kirsch, Barbara and Joseph Lengermann. "An Empirical Test of Robert Blauner's Ideas on Alienation in Work as Applied To Different Type Jobs in a White-Collar Setting," *Sociology and Social Research,* 56, January 1972, pp. 180-194.

Kohn, Melvin. "Occupational Structure and Alienation," *American Journal of Sociology,* 82, July 1976, pp. 111-130.

Kornhauser, Arthur. *Mental Health of the Industrial Worker*. New York: John Wiley and Sons, 1965.

Kovarik and Devolites. *Employee Stock Ownership Plans and the Economic Development Administration*. Washington: National Suggestion Box, November 8, 1977.

Laumann, Edward and Franz Pappi. *Networks of Collective Action*. New York: Academic Press, 1976.

Lawler, E.E. "Reward Systems." In *Improving Life at Work*. J.R. Hackman and J.L. Suttle, eds. Santa Monica, CA: Goodyear, 1977.

Lefebvre, Henri. *The Sociology of Marx*. Harmondsworth, Middlesex, England: Penguin Books, 1972.

Leibenstein, Harvey. "Allocative Efficiency vs. X-Efficiency," *American Economic Review,* June 1966.

Liu, Ben-Chieh. *Quality of Life Indicators in U.S. Metropolitan Areas*. New York: Praeger, 1976.

Long, Norton E. "The Corporation, Its Satellites in the Local Community," in *The Corporation in Modern Society.* Edward S. Mason, ed. Cambridge, MA: Harvard University Press, 1959, pp. 202-217.

Long, Richard J. "The Effect of Employee Ownership on Organization, Employee Job Attitudes and Organization Performance: A Tentative Framework and Empirical Findings," *Human Relations,* January 1978, pp. 29-48.

Management and Economic Research, Inc. *Industrial Location as a Factor in Regional Economic Development.* Washington: Government Printing Office. Undated.

Manuso, James. "Coping With Job Abolishment," *Journal of Occupational Medicine,* 19, 9, September 1977, pp. 598-602.

McCarthy, John and Mayer Zald. "Resource Mobilization and Social Movements: A Partial Theory," *American Journal of Sociology,* 82, May 1977, pp. 1212-1242.

McNulty, James E. "A Test of the Time Dimension in Economic Base Analysis," *Land Economics,* 53, 3, August 1977, pp. 359-368.

The Measurement of Corporate Social Performance, New York: American Institute of Certified Public Accountants, 1977.

Melman, Seymour. "Industrial Efficiency Under Managerial Versus Cooperative Decision-Making." In *Self-Governing Socialism,* 2. Branko Horvat, M. Markovic, and R. Supek, eds. White Plains, NY: International Arts and Sciences Press, Inc., 1975, pp. 203-220.

Mesazaros, Istvan. *Marx's Theory of Alienation.* New York: Harper and Row, 1972.

Mick, Stephen S. "Social and Personal Costs of Plant Shutdowns," *Industrial Relations,* 14, 2, May 1975, pp. 203-208.

Michelson, Stephan. *Community Based Development in Urban Areas.* Cambridge, MA: Center for Community Economic Development, October 14, 1977, mimeo.

Mishan, Edward J. *Cost-Benefit Analysis.* New York: Praeger, 1976.

Muller, Thomas. "Growth Cycles and Costs of Growth," in *Post-Industrial America: Metropolitan Decline and Inter-Regional Job Shifts*. George Sternlieb and J.W. Hughes, eds. New Brunswick, NJ: The Center for Urban Policy Research, Rutgers-The State University of New Jersey, 1975, pp. 265-266.

Nord, Walter R. "The Failure of Current Applied Behavioral Science: A Marxian Perspective," *Journal of Applied Behavioral Science*, 10, 1974, pp. 557-578.

Nord, Walter R. "Some Questions and Comments About Approaches to Job Satisfaction." Unpublished paper presented at a meeting of the Academy of Management, New Orleans, August 1975.

Oberschall, Anthony. *Social Conflict and Social Movements*. Englewood Cliffs, NJ: Prentice-Hall, Inc., 1973.

Olson, Mancur Jr. "Economics, Sociology and the Best of All Possible Worlds," *The Public Interest*, 12, Summer 1968, pp. 96-118.

Pellegrin, Roland J. and C.H. Coates. "Absentee-Owned Corporations and Community Power Structure," *American Journal of Sociology*, 51, March 1956, pp. 413-417.

Prest, A.R. and R. Turvey. "Cost-Benefit Analysis: A Survey," *Economic Journal*, 75, 300, December 1965, pp. 683-735.

Recard, Richard H. Jr. "The Assignment of Equity Ownership and Its Effect on the Satisfaction of Psychosocial Needs in the Labor Managed Community," paper presented to the Second International Conference on Self-Management, June 1975, Cornell University, Ithaca, NY.

Salancik, Gerald R. and J. Pfeffer. "A Social Information Process Approach to Job Attitudes and Task Design," *Administrative Science Quarterly*, 23, 2, 1978, pp. 224-253.

Schumpeter, Joseph A. *Capitalism, Socialism and Democracy*. 3rd edition. New York: Harper and Brothers, 1950.

Selye, Hans. "Stress and Disease," *Science*, 122, 1955, pp. 625-631.

Shelton, John P. "Allocative Efficiency vs. X-Efficiency: Comment," *American Economic Review*, 57, 5, December 1967, pp. 1252-1258.

Shultz, George P. and A.R. Webster. *Strategies for the Displaced Worker*. New York: Harper and Row, 1966.

Slote, Alfred. *Shutdown: Termination at Baker Plant.* Indianapolis: Bobbs-Merrill, 1969.

Smith, Luke A. and I.A. Fowler. "Plant Relocation and Worker Migration." In *Blue-Collar World: Studies of the American Worker.* Arthur B. Shostak and W. Gomberg, eds. Englewood Cliffs, NJ: Prentice-Hall, 1964, pp. 491-497.

Somers, Gerald G. and W.D. Wood. *Cost-Benefit Analysis of Manpower Policies.* Kingston, Ontario: Queen's University, 1969.

Stein, Barry A. *Size, Efficiency and Community Enterprise.* Cambridge, MA: Center for Community Economic Development, 1974.

Stigler, George J. "The Xistence of X-Efficiency," *American Economic Review,* 66, 1, March 1976, pp. 213-216.

Strange, Walter G. "Job Loss: A Psychosocial Study of Worker Reactions to a Plant-Closing in a Company Town in Southern Appalachia." Ph.D. dissertation, Cornell University, 1977.

The Measurement of Corporate Social Performance. New York: American Institute of Certified Public Accountants, 1977.

United States Code, 1940 Edition. Washington: Government Printing Office, p. 2964.

U.S. Department of Health, Education and Welfare. *Work in America.* Cambridge, MA: MIT Press, 1973.

Valenta, Frank. Testimony before the Committee on Ways and Means. Ohio State Senate, Columbus, OH, February 14, 1968.

Vroom, Victor H. *Work and Motivation.* New York: John Wiley and Sons, 1964.

Wall Street Journal, August 16, 1976.

Ward, Ian D.S. and J.C.G. Wright. *An Introduction to Market Capitalism.* Melbourne, Australia: Longmar Cheshire, PIC, 1977.

Warren, Roland L. "Toward a Man-Utopian Normative Model of the Community," *American Sociological Review,* 35, April 1970, pp. 219-228.

Weiss, Carol H. *Evaluation Research.* Englewood Cliffs, NJ: Prentice-Hall, 1972.

Whitman, Edmund S. and W.J. Schmidt. *Plant Relocation: A Case History of a Move.* New York: American Management Association, 1966.

Wilcock, Richard C. and W.H. Franke. *Unwanted Workers.* New York: Free Press, 1963.

5
Cost-Benefit
Analysis: Economic

In this chapter, community-employee purchase of firms, as a means to maintain and create jobs, is evaluated through a cost-benefit analysis of the Mohawk Valley Community Corporation purchase of the Library Bureau. The criterion in this form of evaluation is whether or not the ratio of benefits to costs, as seen at the time of the purchase decision, is greater than one.

Cost-benefit analysis generally requires consideration of the feasible alternative courses of action. Two basic alternatives will be analyzed here:

(1) purchase and operation of the plant under conditions of community-employee ownership;
(2) complete shutdown of the Library Bureau, as planned by the Sperry Rand Corporation.

No other alternatives were likely. There were no other prospective buyers with sufficient resources.

The costs and benefits are estimated for a five-year period from the date of purchase. Though the five-year period is somewhat arbitrary, it also reflects the possibility that the community will sell its financial interests in the company after several years. Within the field of community economic development, a developing strategy in declining areas is the governmental or quasi-governmental organization of an enterprise which is sold once it has attained viability—that is, a "spin-off" approach. In

117

the particular case of the MVCC, an Employee Stock Ownership Plan has been instituted which may eventually buy many of the shares now held by the community at large rather than by the employees.

There is no assurance that such a stock transfer will occur, but this assumption entails a further differentiation between the evaluation of this particular case and the situation in which the distribution of shares is fixed by the organization's charter. When distributions of ownership are fixed (see Long, 1978), the CEF remains indefinitely owned jointly by the community in general, as well as the employees. Such an arrangement may be quite important because many of the relative advantages of a CEF accrue in the long term. For example, a CEF faced with the need to make a new allocation of capital locally or elsewhere is more likely to invest locally and maintain community jobs because of the basic congruence of interests between corporation and community. In quantifiable cost terms, a long term view increases the favorability of a CEF because the heavy purchase cost is incurred early, whereas the expectation is that the benefits will accrue as long as the company survives. However, the long term effects (beyond five years) are not considered in this part of the evaluation. A relatively short time period is used because of the doubtfulness of predicting the success of enterprises subject to the market, and the intention of providing a conservative estimate of benefits relative to costs.

The analysis assumes that the feasibility studies completed during the decision to purchase the firm[1] are an accurate representation of the expected value[2] of the financial stream of benefits accruing from the continued operation of the plant under the MVCC. It is not the intention of the present study to perform a

---

1. "Preliminary Information for Proposal to Purchase Library Bureau division of Sperry Rand Corporation," Moval Management Corporation, March 31, 1976, mimeo; and Economic Development Administration loan application documents, June 24, 1976, mimeo.

2. The expected value is obtained by assigning probabilities to the possible range of benefits and obtaining a weighted average as the benefit figure. This procedure also makes an adjustment for the perceived riskiness of the project.

full-scale conventional feasibility study of the firm. Such a study is an obvious first step for communities and/or employees considering a plant acquisition, but the techniques are quite well known and do not require repetition here. The feasibility evaluation is taken as a stepping off point and the cost-benefit analysis of the acquisition is made from an unconventional viewpoint—that of the community. Consequently, the presentation of costs and benefits are somewhat different from the usual format. An elaboration of the modifications required in the traditional approach to costs and benefits appears in Appendix A to this chapter.

Much of this analysis relies upon community "economic base theory," a model commonly used by community and regional development economists. This theory posits that a community's economic condition is particularly contingent upon its "basic" or "export" industries (e.g., Duncan and Reiss, 1956), that is, those which market their products outside the community. The development effects of manufacturing industries are especially emphasized, but other community employment and income sources, including agricultural establishments, military bases, and transfer payments, may be part of the base. Early literature (Weimer and Hoyt, 1939) concentrated on establishing ratios of basic to non-basic, or service sector employment and income using only static analysis. Recently, researchers have emphasized differential effects of segments of the base within a dynamic framework (Weiss and Gooding, 1968; Garnick, 1970).

The aims of the theory are the effect of a change in economic base on the provision of services in the area. The effects are categorized as *direct,* that is those immediately associated with the change in the economic base, *indirect,* the immediate interindustry linkage effects, and *induced,* the second and subsequent rounds of effects.

This analysis treats the likely direct and indirect community loss of wage and salary income and the estimated loss of income from locally-supplied raw materials, resulting from a Library Bureau shutdown, as a decrease in the community's base-related income.

The estimated losses in these items which were avoided through the CEF are shown as benefits in table 5-1. The losses would also have had negative induced effects, and the estimate of avoided induced loss is also shown as a benefit. Further discussion of the model behind these estimates is given in the list of benefits which follows and in Appendix A to this chapter.

Costs and benefits are assessed from the viewpoint of the community[3] because we regard it as the decision making entity primarily relevant to creating employment through the development of CEFs. Other possible levels of analysis which could be used include the societal, the governmental, and the individual. A societal viewpoint is the traditional ideal because it would include the effects on all persons in society, rather than just a subsection. An evaluation from the view of the federal government is of relevance because plant shutdown costs of increased social service payments, lost tax payments, increased support of local governments, etc. may be incurred at this level, and because communities are likely to look for federal help to develop CEFs. Individuals faced with job loss due to shutdowns need to assess whether their resources are better allocated to saving their jobs through a CEF or to alternatives such as relocation, retraining or savings. However, this unique strategy is directed toward community welfare and must first be evaluated from that perspective. Other actors in the social system (government, individuals) must also evaluate this strategy in accordance with their own interests.

The analysis presented in this chapter is based upon the set of assumptions regarding relevant factors, estimated values, and discount rates which seems most plausible. However, a variety of estimates must be made and there is little opportunity to test their precision except within some range of values. The sensitivity of the

---

3. Community is defined in both territorial and functional terms. Territorially, it is the inhabitants of the contiguous towns of Herkimer, Mohawk, Ilion, and the village of Herkimer. An additional criterion of significant functional ties enabled the inclusion of firm employees not resident in the above community and farmers and loggers who provide the firm's main raw material and operate in the hinterlands of Herkimer (see chapter 2).

evaluation to variations in the range of values a factor may take is considered in a separate analysis presented after the main results.

A discount rate of 6 percent is used in the main text, and results are also shown for 3 percent and 15 percent rates in the sensitivity analysis. A discount rate is applied in cost-benefit analysis because people generally prefer income now rather than later. For example, benefits of a project received in the future must be reduced to their perceived worth to the decision maker at the time the decision is being made. The benefits are discounted to their present value using a rate which reflects the opportunity cost to the decision maker if the funds were invested in the next best alternative. The choice of a 6 percent rate and the method of dealing with price changes are discussed more fully in Appendix A. In brief, constant prices and a discount rate adjusted for expectations of inflation were used.

The analysis is done as if the community had undertaken it at the time of the shutdown threat. Basing calculations and judgments upon information available and conditions prevailing at that time provides an illustration of how other communities might carry out such a study. The beginning date for the five-year evaluation period is August 1, 1976.

The cost and benefit factors in the whole evaluation are categorized as either (1) economic; or (2) "social," that is, psychological, psychophysiological, sociological, and political.[4] The economic results covered in this chapter are presented as follows: (a) quantified (monetarily valued) benefits; (b) quantified costs; (c) non-quantified benefits; and (d) non-quantified costs.

---

4. The term "social" is not fully satisfactory because, in the cost-benefit analysis literature, it customarily refers to taking a national or society viewpoint. However, the only apparent alternative, "non-economic," has the connotation that these factors are in a sub-category and of lesser significance. An emphasis of this study is that evaluations such as this must give full significance to factors beyond the economic. Consequently, "social" will be used here, despite its deficiencies. The national perspective is referred to here by employing the term "societal."

The quantified benefits and costs are summarized in tables 5-1, 5-2, and 5-3. As previously discussed, the results show the present value of the costs and benefits from the viewpoint of the community over a five-year period using a 6 percent rate of discount. The present values have been calculated as if all cost and benefit payments after the initial date occur in lump sums at the end of each of the five yearly periods. This procedure aids calculations and, as all items are treated consistently, will not substantially affect the relative magnitudes of the costs and benefits.Grant, Ireson, and Leavenworth's (1976) standard text on cost-benefit analysis argued that complete precision is unnecessary as long as an accurate representation is provided of the costs and benefits, especially when significant factors in the decision making are not reducible to monetary values.

The wage and salary estimates have been adjusted for federal and state income tax payments and social security deductions. Twenty percent was deducted from the wages projected for MVCC lower level employees and 25 percent for top management. Roughly proportional lower reductions were made in the estimates of the incomes former Library Bureau employees would have obtained if the plant had been closed. Similar adjustments were made for other persons whose wage incomes would have been directly affected by a shutdown.

QUANTIFIED ECONOMIC BENEFITS

Direct Wage and Salary Income

The difference between an estimate of the wage and salary income stream of the MVCC employees, given that the company operates as predicted, and the income stream of the former Library Bureau employees, if the plant had shut down, was calculated. The total represents the avoided loss to the community of the wage and salary income, i.e., a benefit.

The MVCC income stream was estimated using the September 1976 employment and wage and salary levels as bases, and assuming a 5 percent rise per year in each. The September 1976 local employment was 250. Based on detailed payroll information made available, a 1976 mean annual wage level of $9,100 was computed for 240 of the employees. The mean annual salary level for 10 top management was calculated to be $20,201. The gross wages and salaries are adjusted downward to account for the portion of them which flow out of the community as income taxes and social security deductions.

The income stream if the plant had not continued through community-employee ownership was much more complicated to calculate. Information on the probable labor market experience of terminated Library Bureau employees was obtained from federal and New York State Department of Labor reports pertinent to the Utica-Rome SMSA market.[5] Sunday editions of a major local newspaper for the September 1976-September 1977 period were scanned to ascertain job openings not notified to the Department of Labor. Current MVCC employees were surveyed to establish if they were aware of any local job openings in the woodworking industry at the time of the proposed plant shutdown, and to estimate the likelihood that a worker expected to have to move away from the community.

The extensive labor economics literature on plant closures (summarized in Haber, Ferman and Hudson, 1963 and Holen, 1976) was reviewed to aid the estimate. Using this information plus knowledge of the skill, tenure, and demographic characteristics of the employees, and the technology and size of the backlog orders of the firm, estimates were made of the likely labor market experiences of former Library Bureau employees. Six major employee subgroups were used, primarily categorized according to occupational group and date of termination, in addition to a projection of the likely experiences within each subgroup. These estimates formed the basis of the projected income stream into the

---

5. *Labor Area Summary* (formerly *Manpower Review*), January 1975-September 1978, Vol. II No. 1-Vol. II No. 9; *JOBFLO: A Report on Demand Occupations, Utica-Rome,* August 1977; *Applicants and Openings, Utica-Rome Metropolitan Area,* May 1977; *Hiring Specifications, New York State,* May 1977, pp. 79-91; *Employment and Earnings,* September 1976-September 1977; *Characteristics of the Insured Unemployed, Utica-Rome Area,* April-June 1977.

community if the plant had closed. The likelihood of obtaining unemployment insurance benefits, pensions, social security payments, withdrawing from the workforce, and relocating were all taken into account.

Unlike a study utilizing a societal or governmental level of analysis, unemployment insurance benefits and social security payments were not treated as a loss resulting from the plant closure. From a community point of view, such benefits and payments are a positive addition to its income stream when employees become unemployed or retire. Conversely, the income that persons forced to relocate by the plant closure would have received in the community if it had not shut down is regarded as a loss. Different levels of analysis can reverse these treatments or disregard them as being only transfer effects.

In present value terms adjusted for taxes and deductions, the total wage and salary income obtained within the community by the MVCC employees if the plant continues operations as expected (direct MVCC income) is $8,788,853. The comparable figure if the plant had closed and the former Library Bureau employees had to obtain income through alternative employment or other means (direct non-MVCC income) is $5,616,731. The difference between these is $3,172,122, and this is the amount entered into table 5-1 as a benefit. The non-MVCC direct income represents a 36 percent loss compared to continued operation of the plant under community-employee ownership.

Sixty-three percent of the estimated direct wage and salary income loss of $3,172,122 is a result of the relocation of 57 persons outside the community. The other portion of the loss is the decreased income suffered by the persons who remained and became unemployed, were employed at lower wage rates, withdrew from the workforce, or retired early relying upon pensions and social security benefits. The average income loss for these former employees who remained in the community is approximately 17 percent. This aggregate figure masks wide variations. For example, the calculations assume that the younger professional employees who remain suffer little or no income loss, whereas many of the older workers with few skills or industry-specific skills incur losses in the range of 30 percent.

The calculations are illustrated using the unskilled and semi-skilled production workers as an example. Based primarily on knowledge of the firm's technology and amount of backlog at the time of the shutdown announcement, 32 unskilled and 8 semi-skilled, relatively low tenure younger employees, would have been terminated at the beginning of August, 1976. Utilizing Department of Labor statistics on the conditions in the local labor market, the economic literature on plant closures, and worker estimates which roughly confirm the figures, the following changes would occur:

(1) 10 terminated employees would leave the community;
(2) 7 would have income of 4 weeks of unemployment insurance (at $95.00 per week) and obtain employment for the remainder of the 5-year evaluation period at a wage level 10 percent lower than they would have obtained if the MVCC maintained their jobs (5 percent overall loss compared to MVCC income stream);
(3) 13 would receive 26 weeks of unemployment insurance and have wage losses in their jobs of 10 percent relative to the MVCC (7 percent loss);
(4) 10 would have 52 weeks of unemployment insurance and experience 15 percent relative wage losses (13 percent loss).

The assumed relative wage losses take into account (1) the common occurrence of terminated employees experiencing several temporary jobs before being able to obtain steady income; (2) a downward adjustment to recognize the higher riskiness and thus, lower expected value of the chances of former Library Bureau employees obtaining employment through the labor market compared to the riskiness of the alternative MVCC income; (3) the week-long waiting period(s) experienced before unemployment insurance payments can be obtained; and (4) increased commuting costs for those who do not relocate, but are forced to work outside the community.

Similar calculations were performed for other subgroups but different conditions were assumed for some subgroups and sections of subgroups. For example, it was assumed that a lower proportion of the older, blue-collar employees would relocate, compared to the group just described, but a higher proportion of top management and professional personnel would leave. Further details are given in Appendix B. The sensitivity analysis which follows presents results using alternative assumptions for these calculations.

Indirect Income

The MVCC's loan application to the Economic Development Administration states that 36 local jobs would be directly affected by a Library Bureau shutdown—15 in sawmills, 15 in logging crews, 3 security guards, and 3 cleaners. These figures assume that the lumber industry is able to largely adjust and find new markets, but does experience some downturn. Consequently, the calculations are made under the assumption that 10 jobs are eliminated as a direct result of the LB shutdown. If this occurred, and these workers had similar unemployment and reemployment experiences as the former LB workers, the community would have sustained a loss of $112,873, in present value terms over the five years.

Local Purchases of Raw Materials

This item is comprised of the likely avoided losses related to the plant's purchases of locally obtained logs and sawn lumber. Approximately $625,000 is paid out locally to logging crews who obtain the wood under contracts with farmers, and lumber yards who purchase wood locally through direct contracts with farmers.

Though loss of income to logging crews has been counted, the loss of the Library Bureau's purchases would have depleted the income of local farmers and lumber merchants. There are other industrial wood-users in the vicinity, but they would not have increased demand to compensate for the LB closure, and the competitors of LB are too distant from Herkimer to directly replace the lost demand. Information from the company suggests that only the close vicinity of the plant made wood-selling economically sensible for farmers who generally have only small stocks of lumber.

Nevertheless, lumber dealers assume that some market for the wood could have been found, especially if lower prices were accepted and higher transportation costs absorbed. A 20 percent loss is estimated over the evaluation period compared to maintaining the plant through a CEF. (The sensitivity analysis assumes a 10 percent loss.)

Other Local Purchases

The company estimates that $50,000 per year is spent locally on construction and maintenance work, advertising, office materials, vehicles, and other minor purchases. Eighty percent of this has been included as an avoided loss. The underlying assumption is that these procurements can only be sold locally and that their only substitutes are other locally produced and sold goods, rather than goods which are imports from the community viewpoint. If the sellers to the LB lowered their prices subsequent to a shutdown, and the presumed increase in volume sold enabled them to recoup their losses, the shift in market constitutes a transfer of community income to purchases of these goods instead of others sold by the community. That is, the loss has simply been transferred.

Induced Income

Economic base theory suggests that a change in a community's export-related employment and income will have a direct multiplier effect. A plant closure depletes a community's stock of jobs even if those workers directly affected are able to be reemployed. A type of "bumping-down" process occurs. The effect is reduced by "leakages" in the form of relocations, workforce withdrawals, and switches from community to non-community jobs, but is still substantial, especially in a community where the supply of jobs is stagnant or even declining.

For example, workers first entering the labor force are more likely to leave the community and women who might otherwise have joined the workforce do not do so. There is a net loss in community employment.

The decline in export income also has effects through lowering sales of service firms and of "second round" and subsequent suppliers (i.e., beyond those shown in the above sections as direct and indirect effects). The induced income item estimates the cumultive effects of these processes. As rated previously, a description of this model and its application to the analysis is provided in Appendix A.

Net Value of Assets

An additional item is included to account for the possibility that community owners may sell the plant to a non-community owner after five years. The benefit realized at that point is valued by estimating the market price obtainable for the enterprise less the cost of the EDA and bank loans still payable.The price paid to Sperry Rand by the community is the best estimate of the market price obtainable, that is, $4,663,000. This figure assumes that the disbenefit to be deducted is the amount which would have been paid if the buyer took over the same loan payments. This is the most likely occurrence. The reasoning behind treating loans payable as a disbenefit rather than a cost and the results using the latter alternative are shown in the sensitivity analysis. Concern over the interest of community members in relinquishing local control is considered in chapter 9.

The six economic benefits detailed above are summarized in the following table.

Table 5-1
Quantified Economic Benefits

Benefits	Present Value $
Direct wage and salary income............	3,172,122
Indirect income	112,873
Local purchases of raw materials...........	526,500
Other local procurements	168,480
Induced income	1,057,466
Net value of assets	1,933,825
Total	6,971,266

Shareholders Equity

The MVCC first *Annual Report* states that the company had raised net proceeds of $1,584,452 from the sale of short term notes and common stock to enable the acquisition of the Library Bureau. Using the economist's concept of opportunity cost, the true cost of this outlay to the community is the income which it foregoes through this amount being invested in the MVCC. If it is assumed that the community would have obtained a return from this sum at a 12 percent per annum rate, then the cost of this outlay is $950,671 over the five years, or $800,845 in present value terms. The sensitivity analysis presents results utilizing a somewhat higher opportunity cost.

Acquisition Campaign Expenses

Community businessmen donated approximately $15,000 into a fund designated as a "War Chest," to provide working capital for the campaign to save the plant. The Herkimer County Legislature Proceedings for 1976 reports that the executive director of the Mohawk Valley Economic Development District, Inc. requested an extra $3,000 funding for his organization due to unusual costs resulting from the campaign to save the Library Bureau. Descriptions of the community drive to obtain the acquisition note many meetings and communications of local businessmen, politicians, and other influential persons, as well as much voluntary work by union officers and company executives and their wives. A somewhat arbitrary valuation of $2,000 is placed on this activity. The total campaign costs are thus estimated to be $20,000.

Again, using the concept of opportunity cost and an alternative return of 12 percent, the real cost to the community of the campaign is $10,019 in present value.

Loans

A total of $3.6 million was obtained through four promissory notes held by the Economic Development Administration and two banks in Utica. The yearly amounts of principal and interest payable over five years was calculated and converted into present values. These economic costs of the plant purchase are summarized in table 5-2.

Table 5-2
Quantified Economic Costs

Costs	Present Value
Shareholders equity.....................	$ 800,845
Acquisition campaign expenses	10,108
Loans	2,250,016
Total	$3,060,969

The ratio of the benefits and costs covered above is given in table 5-3. It shows that (in present value terms) the benefits total of $6,971,266 is more than twice the costs figure of $3,060,969.

Table 5-3
Comparison of Quantified Economic Benefits and Costs

Benefits	Present Value $
Direct wage and salary income.............	3,172,122
Indirect income	112,873
Local purchases of raw materials...........	526,500
Other local procurements	168,480
Induced income	1,057,466
Net value of assets	1,933,825
Total	6,971,266

Costs	Present Value $
Shareholders equity......................	800,845
Acquisition campaign expenses	10,108
Loans	2,250,016
Total	3,060,969
Benefit:Cost Ratio.......................	2.28:1

SENSITIVITY ANALYSIS

The aim of this additional analysis is to show how alterations in major and problematic parameters can change the cost-benefit results. One such parameter is the discount rate. Results follow which are derived using 3 percent and 15 percent rates, as well as the 6 percent rate chosen as the best estimate.

There are a multitude of conceivable permutations of this analysis for which benefit-cost ratios could be obtained. However, the aim of sensitivity analysis, unless being used to compare across separate projects, is to establish whether the ratio becomes less than unity within a plausible range of variation in the project's components. This analysis presents results of a theoretical "worst case" estimation. That is, the most unfavorable figures from the viewpoint of finding a ratio favorable to the CEF alternative are used. This estimation employs the lower bound assumptions regarding benefits and the highest possible estimates with respect to costs. Within this format, the use of parameter values between those of the most likely case and the worst case values is only required if a benefit-cost ratio of less than 1 was found in the worst case; no such ratio was found.

The analyses also assume that the loans payable item is a cost, rather than a disbenefit, as in the main text; elaboration follows the table.

Table 5-4
Sensitivity Analysis

Assumed Cases	Discount Rates		
	3%	6%	15%
1. Most likely case	2 . 19 : 1	2 . 28 : 1	2 . 23 : 1
2. Loans payable as a cost	1 . 73 : 1	1 . 85 : 1	1 . 96 : 1
3. Worst case	1 . 34 : 1	1 . 41 : 1	1 . 48 : 1

Most Likely Case

This is simply the same analysis as given in the main text except that the results using 3 percent and 15 percent discount rates throughout are also shown.

Loans Payable as a Cost

The classification of loans payable as a disbenefit was made through interpolation of the rule-of-thumb that outlays by the entity implementing a project are costs, whereas benefit-reducing effects borne by the general public are treated as disbenefits. Classification in this case is complicated by the high overlap between the operating entity and the general public. Lowering the final "salvage value" benefit by the amount of loans payable is different from counting costs incurred initially or during current operations of the plant under community-employee ownership. Recognizing that this choice is debatable, the ratios presented employ the alternative classification, with all else remaining unchanged.

Worst Case

For this analysis, minimized estimates of benefits, and maximized estimates of costs were calculated. As one aspect of this adjustment, the likely post-shutdown experiences of the former LB employees were seen in the most optimistic light justifiable, lowering the relative benefit of the CEF alternative. By lowering the assumed lengths of unemployment spells, etc., the total community loss for the 40 workers terminated in September, 1976 was decreased, in present value terms, at a 6 percent discount rate, from $442,257 to $350,460. For the 10 member top management group, the worst case (for the purchase) assumes that only 2 would leave the community subsequent to closure, that 6 would be able to obtain local jobs providing the same income, and that 2 others would also obtain local jobs, but with 20 percent income losses overall. In the main text case, the numbers assumed were 6, 3, and 1, respectively (for reasons which are given in Appendix B). The worst case assumptions regarding top management result in a benefit of $147,274, compared to the most likely case amount of $302,779 (using the 6 percent discount rate).

Similar downward adjustments in wage and salary benefits of the CEF were made for other directly and indirectly affected employment. Lumber sellers were able to replace 90 percent of the export-related income previously obtained through the Library Bureau, compared to the earlier assumption of 80 percent. The replacement proportion for the other procurements item was increased from 20 percent to 40 percent.

The estimated sale price of the firm at the end of the evaluation period remains unchanged in this analysis. This figure is a best estimate for which an alternative projection would be too arbitrary, as the only data available is the previous sale price. The worst case continues to treat the loans payable as a cost rather than a disbenefit as in the main text.

134

The induced income benefit was calculated employing the same model, but with a greatly reduced export-income drop measuring the exogenous change. This resulted in lowering the induced benefit by 44 percent.

The cost figures were increased by assuming the equity and campaign-related resources had an opportunity cost equal to those resources obtaining a 15 percent return in alternative uses, compared to the 12 percent earlier used. The cost of loans already paid is actual—not estimated—and is unchanged in the analysis. The costs side in this case is substantially increased by including loans payable.

NON-QUANTIFIED ECONOMIC BENEFITS

This section includes economic effects which were not able to be quantified within the scope of the study. The lack of quantification in no way diminishes their significance to the evaluation. On the contrary, the benefits analyzed here regarding local taxes and, especially, the gain in community control of its economic base are of major community significance.

Property Tax Benefits

One likely result of the closure is a reduction in the real estate taxes paid to the village for the land and buildings of the closed down plant. However, a precise accounting of this loss is quite difficult. Despite the closure, Sperry Rand would still initially have been liable for the same taxes. The taxes are based on the assessed value of the land and buildings and whether or not a business is operating, is, in theory, irrelevant. There may even be a short term gain to the community government. Revenue would be the same with fewer people and lower demand for some services.

Nevertheless, in general, a cessation of operations in a large old plant in an economically depressed region is likely to lead to lower tax revenue from the property.

There are several ways in which this can occur. A comparable case is provided by the shutdown several years earlier of another old woodworking company in the village of Herkimer, the Standard Desk Company factory. In that case, the company made an agreement to pay only a portion of its tax liability (10 percent in the first year of the agreement) because of its poor financial condition. Payments occurred for two years (fiscal years 1973-75) but then Standard Desk was unable to continue, and the property became owned by the local industrial development agency. Property owned by the agency is tax exempt. The site and building have remained unused over the past few years.

This type of process is common in depressed areas with little or no growth and few, if any, buyers. The polar example is commercial building and housing abandonment in ghetto areas. Admittedly, complete abandonment is unlikely in Herkimer, although there are examples in the region in the nearby city of Little Falls. Sperry Rand would not want the adverse publicity of an abandonment and is completely capable of maintaining tax payments. However, the corporation is unlikely to be content with continuing outlays when the property has ceased to provide income.

Whitman and Schmidt (1966) have published a case study guide to appropriate corporate policy for plant relocations. They suggest that a preferable move in a case such as this is to sell the property to the community at a bargain price or even give it away. They mention tax loss advantages and a public relations gain. The community obtains a property, but it represents a loss if the property is placed in a tax exempt category or it sits unsold and undeveloped. Even if a buyer is found or some other form of development occurs, new businesses in such situations are regularly given tax breaks.

The problem of tax exemptions on property is important to communities such as Herkimer. In 1977, the total assessed value of property in the village was $27,893,743, but exemptions totalled to $14,663,347.[6] The resulting tax base is only 47 percent of the total assessment. The (varying) exemptions the village is obliged to give

---

6. Interview with Felicia Griffen, Clerk of the Village of Herkimer.

include those for property owned by local, state and federal governments, schools, veterans, fraternal and church organizations, Herkimer County Industrial Development Agency, Penn-Central Railroad, and the homes of citizens over 65 and veterans. The loss of revenue-producing properties, such as the Standard Desk or the Library Bureau, is a crucial component of the shrinking tax base often discussed with regard to communities in the Northeast.

If, instead of the property reverting to the village in some manner, Sperry sold the machinery and other equipment (as it intended), and sold the property separately, it would have been for a low price. The low value placed on it by the market would encourage a request for lowered assessment. If the property had simply been left over the five-year period of this analysis, then vandalism and other deterioration would have occurred resulting in lower property tax revenue. The complex options prevent any adequate estimate of the property tax loss to the village. Nevertheless, some cost was likely and has been avoided by saving the plant.

Plant closure also has substantial impact on property taxes collected by the village because of forced migration and other lowered community direct income effects. However, transferred effects remain important. Net out-migration would have lowered village property tax collections by the amount these emigrants would have paid (all else being equal). This loss is not an additional loss to the community beyond the migration-related direct income loss because the local tax payments are only a transfer of community income.

Those who remained and suffered direct income losses would also suffer losses in the value of their housing over the five-year period because the economy of the area was unlikely to grow. The demand for new homes and incentives for home improvement would be likely to decline and actual deterioration could occur. The effects may have produced some land or housing abandonment or an inability to meet the tax obligations. The minimum likely effect is a lower rate of growth in assessed value of community property owned by those directly affected. In contrast, the community members not directly affected face the prospect of higher taxes. Lower tax collections because of abandonments or lower assessments implies lower services or increased rates. Either imposes a cost on persons not directly affected by the shutdown. However, this is not an additional cost in cost-benefit analysis terms. The increased payments or lowered services suffered by those not directly affected represent a spreading of the direct income loss already included.

A similar argument applies in principle to property tax payments to the school district. Both have the same tax assessment basis, but the school system is subject to different regulations and the process of loss differs. In addition, state aid, which provides 63 percent of the district's estimated revenues for 1977-78, is primarily based on weighted daily average attendance. If a plant closure results in pupil loss, then less state aid is received, producing a community income loss. Fewer students means less demand for services, but school systems generally have fixed costs which cannot be quickly adjusted downward because of lower revenues. Of course, the situation is actually more complex. For example, New York State had a "hold-safe" law under which no school district could obtain less state aid than in the previous year. However, this law has now been changed in the face of declining enrollments, and other states do not have such guarantees. The complexities again prevent confident estimate of real losses. Nevertheless, the general observation that poorer areas with declining and weak tax bases generally have lower quality school systems can be applied. The community avoided costs to its school system through saving the plant with community-employee ownership.

Planning Benefits

Because the LB will remain in the community and greater information is now locally available on its operation, local development agencies and governments have received the substantial benefit of improved planning capabilities. Community investments in infrastructure are generally long term, and mis-estimates can be very costly. An example within the same SMSA is the city of Rome's allocation of resources for a new road and educational facilities under the assumption that the nearby air force base would maintain approximately the same workforce. When a major cutback was unexpectedly announced, one objection of the city was that its infrastructural investment would be wasted. To the extent that community control of its economic base enables better projections of service requirements, the CEFs provide an additional fiscal benefit to the community.

Similar considerations apply to individual planning. Obviously, the likelihood of certain jobs being available is crucial to individual decision making regarding investments in skills, home-buying, etc. All such long term choices are less likely to go awry the more reliably future employment can be predicted.

Economic Base Benefits

Previous sections evaluated benefits by illustrating what might have happened economically to the community if the plant had ceased operations. Studies pursuing the same approach have shown that, beyond the direct income loss effects, communities which experience permanent major losses of employment are afflicted, after some lag, by a downward multiplier effect. Complex chains of negative interactions occur; for example, a plant closes, the community loses income and people, a dwindling population has to pay higher local tax rates or services decline, these latter occurrences result in more persons and firms leaving, the community loses more income . . . and so on. Similar chains could be shown for other economic factors. In extreme cases, the community becomes a ghost town. More commonly, because of economic stabilizing and counteracting forces (such as government transfers) and because the people affected by plant closures are generally immobile, the community stabilizes at a lower level of welfare, rather than spiraling ever downward. Lantz (1971) reports that sweatshop-type industries developed after the coal mines declined in Coaltown, and similar developments occurred in old textile mill towns in New England. After Sperry Rand closed its Univac plant it Utica in early 1977, the only local employer offering significant numbers of similar jobs was non-union and paid substantially lower than the machinists union-organized Univac.[7]

Awareness of this process of community decline is common. The problem is to stop it or to obtain the means of adjusting the rate to one in accord with a full accounting of the costs and benefits involved. A major benefit of a CEF is that it provides a means by which a community can adjust the rate of change of its economic institutions in conformity with the community's preferences (although still, of course, basically subject to market constraints). Social and economic change may occur gradually and avoid some of the traumatic events of rapid changes.

NON-QUANTIFIED ECONOMIC COSTS

The significant economic costs of the CEF have been relatively simple to identify in monetary terms, and the costs remaining are few. The single non-quantifiable cost which analysts must consider is that the community's economic future is now more crucially tied to the plant than it was before. If the CEF is not a success, community savings as well as jobs have been lost. The consequences of this may be worse than the shutdown under normal conditions. The riskiness of having both job and savings dependent on an enterprise must be considered.[8] This especially applies to the employees where there is a high degree of employee ownership. Prominent union leader William Winpinsinger has identified this problem as a major impediment to employee ownership, and most North American and European unions concur with this view.[9] Apart from this noteworthy issue, all major economic costs have been quantified.

---

7. Interview with George Joseph, former president of the International Association of Machinists union local at the Univac plant, March 18, 1978.

8. Inclusion of this risk as a separate cost item can be seen as double-counting. The riskiness of the project has already been taken into account in the income stream projections. However, because of the difficulty of estimating risk and the major importance of this issue, it was judged that this factor required explicit recognition. However, the fear of workers losing everything in vain attempts to salvage non-viable firms is reduced by the CEF approach (compared to solely employee ownership) because the investment and risk is spread community-wide.

9. Interview with George Joseph.

Comparison of Non-Quantified Economic Benefits and Costs

The community has made an important gain in its ability to control its economic future. It has also avoided further erosion of the tax base. Community and employee share-buyers risked resources, but the risk was a calculated one.

The inability to quantify these factors precludes a definitive conclusion. Nevertheless, the benefits discussed here appear to carry more weight than the one additional non-quantified cost. Evaluating these factors, the community-employee decision to purchase the Library Bureau was apparently correct.

APPENDIX A

Cost-Benefit Analysis Format Methodology

The community outlay of approximately $1.6 million maintained the income flow into the community of the firm's total sales revenue. The bulk of this revenue is distributed locally and is shown item by item in the list of benefits (although the benefit figures themselves are actually only the differences between the maintained benefits and what these income flows would be without the CEF). This list of benefits does not account for all the distribution of revenue, and allocations to non-local beneficiaries take most of the remainder. Examples of such items are the principal and interest payments on the loans, which are included in the list of costs, payments to a non-local utility company, corporate taxes paid to governments outside the community, and salaries paid to non-local employees, all of which are excluded from the table of cost items.

A more conventional feasibility study would list these latter three items as costs, and also show the sales revenue on the credit side. However, the aim of this study and the form of presentation are designed to highlight the costs and benefits to the local community. Consequently, many non-local debits against the gross sales revenue benefit need not be shown. Instead, all CEF community income inflows and outflows not listed in the cost-benefit table are treated as internal operations of the firm which will cancel out except for some small residual (unless the firm breaks even). This residual is not estimated because it is subject to too many unknowns (including accounting decisions within the firm) and is unlikely to be of a size which would significantly affect the cost-benefit analysis results.

Conceptually, this residual affects the net value of the assets item. This item is a type of residual benefit obtained at the end of the evaluation period, generally called "scrap value" or "salvage value" in the language of cost-benefit analysis. If the internal operations residual is positive (as suggested by the local feasibility study), the calculations underestimate the benefits of the CEF because this residual is not added onto the assets, and *vice versa*. The calculations shown implicitly assume that the internal operations debits and credits not presented in the cost-benefit table have a break-even result.

Discount Rate

The 6 percent rate employed is designed to account for inflation. Howe (1971: 55) notes that there are two ways of dealing with future price changes in cost-benefit analysis. One is to predict all relevant price changes and use a market rate of interest as a discount rate. It is assumed that the market rates are adjusted upward in accord with persons' expectations regarding inflation. Alternatively, the analysis can use an assumption of constant prices and a discount rate which does not include an inflation component. For example, if it is thought that the relevant decision maker wants a 14 percent return, but this is partly because he/she expects 8 percent inflation, then a "real" discount rate of 6 percent is appropriate. The latter alternative has been chosen here.

Apart from the inflation rate, the desired rate of return applicable to the resources in this case is dependent on two opposing considerations. First, most of the money outlaid by the community would otherwise have gone into such items as consumer durables, recreation, housing improvements, etc. Consumers, especially those with low- to middle-level incomes, are generally thought to have a high degree of preference for satisfactions now rather than later. This implies that a high rate of return should be applied.

Opposing this view is information from participants in the share-selling campaign. They suggest that many buyers saw their outlay akin to a donation for the general welfare of the community, and expected little or no return. (Reportedly, some of the money was even musty, as if it had been stored away unused.) Reinforcing this understanding of the outlays in the information provided stockholders that, under the provisions of the MVCC loan agreements with the two banks, dividends would not be declared until the loans were repaid (up to seven and a half years). This information suggests a low desired rate of return.

The inflation rate was about 9 percent in 1976, but that was historically high, and the community expectation may have been for a slightly lower rate.

Taking the above points into account, a desired rate of return of 12 percent and a 6 percent inflation rate would be applicable, and thus a 6 percent discount rate applies.

Induced Income

The measured shutdown impact partly reflects economic base and multiplier theory. This literature has concentrated on processes of economic growth. There is a dearth of relevant literature related to community decline, with the exception of the effects of military base closures (Lynch, 1970; Udis, 1973). However, although community decline is not simply the symmetrical opposite of growth, the processes are similar and base theory findings can be utilized.

This analysis relies explicitly on the work of Park (1970), who related monthly base changes to employment and statistically distinguished between interindustry and induced effects, and McNulty (1977), who obtained income multipliers for six segments of the base for seven different time periods. The former author employed data from the St. Louis SMSA; the latter used information from 41 SMSAs in the southeastern United States.

The induced loss occurs through employment and income effects. With respect to employment, the literature on plant closures (in the field of labor economics) has mainly concentrated on losses sustained by the workers directly affected. This approach underestimates negative effects. In Herkimer, many employees terminated by the Library Bureau would not have fared too badly. Looking just at economic factors, the calculations assume that many former LB workers would have obtained other jobs through migrating, commuting, or local opportunities which entailed either little or no loss of income. However, where former LB employees obtained positions which would otherwise have been filled by other community members, the losses to these latter workers need to be taken into account. A bumping-down process would have occurred, resulting in those at the end of the job queue not obtaining employment. Plant closure means a rundown of the community's stock of jobs, a matter especially crucial where there is no offsetting inward flow. This situation is common in relatively static or declining areas such as Herkimer.

The closure-related loss of income results in a downturn of sales in the non-basic sector and a consequent fall in income beyond the initial decline. Community economic base theory attempts to quantify, albeit crudely, these multiple induced effects.

There is considerable debate in the literature on the size of multipliers, the factors affecting their size, the appropriate time lag, the long-run and short-run effects, and other specific points of the theory. The literature in this area suggests a time lag of one year and an induced effect after four years equal to an income multiplier of 1.8. This model was applied to the yearly drops in base sector income which were projected to occur subsequent to a shutdown.

For example, in the first year of the evaluation period (in constant dollars) the community would have experienced an estimated loss of export sector wage and salary income of $665,965, a drop in lumber sales of $125,000, and a drop in other purchases directly linked to the LB valued at $40,000. The multiplier of 1.8 was applied to this total exogenous income decline of $830,965 to show that after four years the community would have experienced an income loss, beyond the initial decline, of $664,772. To obtain present values, this induced loss was apportioned between the four years, in accordance with the results of McNulty (1977).

The export income declines for other years of the evaluation period were treated in the same manner, except, of course, that the reduced effect is calculated for a shorter time because of the period cut-off at five years. For instance, the base income loss in the fourth year is calculated to have only a small ($62,271) induced impact both because it only has one year in which to operate and because within McNulty's model the short term multiplier is minimal.

Appendix B
Labor Market Experiences

The proposed closure of the Library Bureau within one year was announced by Sperry on March 29, 1976. At that time the LB employed 276 personnel. Sperry intended to immediately terminate the 26 field sales representatives, who were scattered throughout the country. As the emphasis of this study is on the community, that is Herkimer and surroundings, the unemployment experience of the sales force is not estimated. This leaves the 250 persons employed actually in Herkimer. The blue-collar, the white-collar, and the management groups are examined in turn.

Blue-Collar Workers

The firm normally operated with a six month to two year time lag between orders taken and the expected delivery. In March 1976 there was a backlog of orders worth $8,011,000, which should be compared with the usual yearly sales of around $12 million. The enterprise normally keeps large stocks of disassembled standard library furniture components which would have been drawn on and not replenished. However, the components still need to be assembled and much of the production consists of non-standard items. The technology involves a stage by stage integrated process. Even in the first stage of the production process, immediate layoffs would have been unlikely because the minimal kiln capacity did not allow a substantial backlog of raw material to be established. (The firm expanded its kiln capacity in 1977.)

The usual blue-collar workforce of about 159 men would have been maintained for six months. After that point the analysis assumes that an initial sharp drop in the workforce would have occurred (September 1976), involving 40 of the lowest seniority men in the early and relatively peripheral parts of the production process. These are younger men, employed in the lesser skilled jobs such as lumber handler, packer, cleaner, and stock clerk.

This hypothetical shutdown schedule further assumes that 54 would have been terminated in December 1976, and that the remaining 65 blue-collar workers all would have lost their jobs in

February 1977. These groups of terminations would have involved, in general, men of successively higher age and skill levels.

White-Collar Workers

With respect to the 81 white-collar, non-management employees
(including 37 women), the staff involved in marketing, design,
order-taking, and some less vital administrative functions would
quickly be eliminated—49 in September, 1976. These would have
been about half women, primarily general office clerks.

Top Management

The projections assume that the ten persons classified as top
management kept their positions until the closure.

Assumed Schedule of Terminations

Appendix table B-1 below shows the LB workforce, at the time
of the proposed closing, divided into occupational and skill-level
groups. The figures are based on payroll data provided by the
company.

Table B-1
Library Bureau Occupational and Skill-Level Groups

1. Blue-collar	
Unskilled	32
Semi-skilled	62
Skilled	58
Foremen	7
	159
2. White-collar	
Office clerical	57
Technicians	9
Professionals	4
Supervisors	11
	81
3. Top management	10
Total	250

A plausible estimate of the schedule of employee separations, based on knowledge of the backlog of orders, the technology, and the occupational groupings is given in the following table.

Table B-2
Terminations Schedule -
Occupational Groups

1. Blue-collar	
September 1976	40
December 1976	54
February 1977	65

2. White-collar	
September 1976	49
February 1977	32

3. Top Management	
February 1977	10

Labor market effects are apparent when the data are rearranged chronologically.

Table B-3
Termination Schedule - Chronological

1. September 1976	
Unskilled blue-collar	32
Semi-skilled blue-collar	8
White-collar	49

2. December 1976	
Semi-skilled blue-collar	54

3. February 1977	
Skilled blue-collar	58
Foremen	7
White-collar	32
Top management	10

Assuming these estimates as a starting point, the likely unemployment experience of the LB employees had the plant been closed is projected.

DATA SOURCES

The two main avenues to be followed in this assessment are area-specific data for the local labor market, and the academic literature on plant shutdowns. Federal and state Department of Labor information on the Utica-Rome SMSA and its subsections[10] allows a detailed picture of the labor market which faced former LB employees and other affected workers. We scanned Sunday editions of a major local newspaper which provided data on job openings not reported to the Department of Labor. A survey of current MVCC employees ascertained knowledge of woodworking industry openings at the time of the proposed closure and estimates of the belief that local jobs were unavailable. Seventeen studies of plant shutdowns between 1929 and 1961 are summarized in *The Impact of Technological Changes* (Haber, Ferman and Hudson, 1963), and another seventeen recent studies condensed in *Losses to Workers Displaced by Plant Closure or Layoff: A Survey of the Literature* (Holen, 1976). Both studies were used to project labor market experiences.

Description of the Utica-Rome Labor Market

The Utica-Rome SMSA labor market over the period in which the LB workers would have become unemployed was dismal. The Department of Labor (DOL) data are a litany of record lows in

---

10. *Utica-Rome Labor Area Summary* (formerly *Manpower Review*), January 1975-September 1978; *JOBFLO: A Report on Demand Occupations, Utica-Rome*, August, 1977; *Applicants and Openings, Utica-Rome Metropolitan Area*, May 1977; *Hiring Specifications, New York State*, May 1977, pp. 79-91; *Annual Planning Report, Fiscal Year 1978, Utica-Rome Labor Area*, June 1977; *Employment and Earnings*, September 1976-September 1977; *Economic Profile, Herkimer County, New York*, Fall 1975. As noted in chapter 1, the relevant labor market is considered to be the whole SMSA. Twenty-eight percent of the Herkimer County labor force commuted to Oneida County (primarily Utica) in 1970.

employment opportunities. Total employment averaged 113,200 in 1976, 5,800 below 1974 and a record low since the data series began in 1970. The manufacturing pay rosters were 30,000 in 1976, a record low in the data series begun in 1958, and a 30 percent drop since 1969. In 1976, the durables goods sector of manufacturing had dropped 34 percent in average employment (10,500 jobs) compared to 1969, and the non-durables employment was at a record low. In February 1977, the predicted month of most LB terminations, manufacturing jobs were at their lowest monthly total since the current data series began in 1958.

The unemployment rate in the SMSA in February 1977 was 12.4 percent. The area's mean 1976 rate was 10.5 percent (range of 10.0-11.9 percent) and the 1977 rate was 9.7 percent (7.3-12.6 percent). The 1976 average quit rate was 0.7 per hundred employees—the lowest in the decade. The ailing condition of the labor market was exacerbated by the shutdown of a Utica plant in the Univac division of Sperry Rand, in early 1977. About 500 workers were terminated in January and another 700 over the next two months. Many of these workers are similar to the LB employees with regard to age and skill and would have been competing with them directly.

The local economy was slow to recover from the recent recession and in 1978, employment opportunities were only slightly improved compared to the record loss in 1976-77. One year after the postulated February 1977 shutdown date, total non-agricultural employment in the SMSA had only risen 6 percent. Manufacturing employment in this period increased only 1,900 jobs, still far below 1974 and late 1960s levels (but an improvement nonetheless). In February 1978, the rate of unemployment (not seasonally adjusted) in the SMSA was 8.6 percent and 9.7 percent in Herkimer County.[11] A national recession, widely predicted for 1979, is likely to have a proportionately worse effect on the Utica-Rome area.

The understanding of the likely labor market experience of former LB and other affected workers was also developed through

---

11. *Utica-Rome Labor Area Summary*, 2, 4, 1978, p. 4, table 1.

examination of more disaggregated data. For example, the Applicants and Openings source, referred to previously, shows that during the October 1, 1976-March 31, 1977 period there were 8,340 persons registered for work in the occupational groups of processing, machine trades, bench work, structural work, and miscellaneous (truck drivers, service station attendants, pack-agers, etc.) compared to 1,566 openings notified to the DOL for these occupations. This is a ratio of 1:5.32 and the DOL suggests that occupations with a ratio of 1:2 or above have a substantial surplus of labor. (This source also provided data on prevailing wage rates.)

The examination of the job opportunities advertised through the local newspaper revealed very few openings related to the woodworking skills possessed by the LB production employees. For lesser-skilled employees, jobs with acceptable wages and conditions were unavailable. White-collar employees would fare somewhat better, especially technicians and those with profes-sional skills. However, the overall and occupation-specific data sources indicated a substantial oversupply for white-collar employees, especially clerical workers. In line with these findings, the survey of current MVCC employees was consistent with these assessments because it showed very little knowledge of alternative job opportunities if the plant had closed.

Findings of Previous Research

Information from the relevant academic literature suggests that laid-off LB employees would have had substantial problems in gaining reemployment, suffered wage rate reductions, and incurred other losses. For example, Jacobson (1975) finds that earnings losses due to a 3 percent employment decline are 65 percent higher if incurred after a period of decreasing employment rather than after a period of increasing or stable employment. Other studies similarly find the state of the labor market crucial, often outweighing the effects of demographic and skill variables (Shultz and Weber, 1966; Haber, Ferman and Hudson, 1963). Small communities are especially sensitive to these effects (Levinson, 1966).

The LB workers would have been forced to enter a labor market sharing the *cumulative* effects of the long term decline in the Northeast, and especially Utica-Rome which was further eroded by the cyclical recessionary downturn which was at its worst through 1975-76. That is, as well as facing no growth in employment opportunities and very few persons voluntarily leaving their jobs, they would have had to compete for scarce jobs with a large number of people who had already been unemployed for substantial periods.

The labor economics literature on job loss shows widely varying subsequent unemployment rates, but it tends to project about 20 percent unemployment one year later. Although the median duration of unemployment tends to be short (less than 10 weeks in Miernyk's study of textile workers, 1955), a number of studies report substantial numbers with extremely long durations, up to and exceeding a year (Bureau of Labor Statistics, 1964; Shultz and Webster, 1966; Tolles, 1966). Most studies show that workers who are older, more tenured, less educated, less skilled, and female tend to suffer the greatest losses. These groups tend to find reemployment more difficult and have larger income reductions. The indications from both the labor market information and comparable academic studies, suggest that a large number of LB workers would experience long term unemployment and suffer substantial wage and other losses.

THE ASSUMED CONDITIONS

Based on this information, as well as knowledge of the skill, tenure, and demographic characteristics of the employees, and technological and size of backlog considerations, the labor market experience of displaced LB workers was simulated. The conditions assumed for the cost-benefit analysis provided in the main text are as follows:

Thirty-two Unskilled and Eight Semi-Skilled Employees Terminated September, 1976

1) 10 terminated employees leave the community immediately after the closure;

2) 7 employees have an income of 4 weeks of unemployment insurance (at $95.00 per week) and obtain employment for the remainder of the 5-year evaluation period at a wage level of 10 percent lower than they had at their LB jobs;

3) 13 receive 26 weeks UI and have wage losses in their jobs of 10 percent relative to the LB;

4) 10 receive 52 weeks UI and experience 15 percent relative wage losses.

Fifty-four Semi-Skilled Employees
Terminated December, 1976

1) 10 leave the community immediately;

2) 44 receive 39 weeks UI and obtain jobs entailing a 15 percent drop in wage income.

Sixty-five Skilled Employees
Terminated February, 1977

1) 10 leave the community;

2) 25 receive UI for 52 weeks, then one year with a pension (25 years service assumed), and subsequently the pension plus social security payments;

3) 30 people obtain UI for 60 weeks, and then have jobs at a 20 percent lower wage.

Forty-nine White-Collar
Terminated September, 1976

1) 9 leave the community;

2) 11 experience one year UI, one year pension only (eleven years service assumed), and the remainder pension plus social security;

3) 13 have 52 weeks UI and then withdraw from the workforce;

4) 16 are paid unemployment insurance for 26 weeks and obtain jobs with a 10 percent relative wage loss.

Thirty-two White-Collar
Terminated February, 1977

1) 12 leave the community;

2) 15 experience 30 weeks UI and a 10 percent wage loss;

3) 5 obtain 52 weeks UI, 30 weeks of a pension only (11 years service) and the remainder obtain social security as well as a pension.

Ten Top Management
Terminated February, 1977

1) 6 leave the community;
2) 3 obtain local jobs at the same pay;
3) 1 obtains a local job but with a 20 percent drop in salary.

These assumptions are only gross approximations. They are estimates of *average* labor market experience over the five-year evaluation period. For example, it is assumed that a subgroup will receive 39 weeks of UI, but this assumption does not suggest that workers will necessarily have a long continuous period of unemployment after the shutdown. The common occurrence for displaced workers is to have several jobs before an adequate one can be found, and thus have several spells of unemployment. The 39 weeks figure is an estimate of the total of these spells. (This implies that different UI pay scales should be used for later unemployment periods. The difficulties of doing so outweigh the benefits.)

Another example is that the percent relative wage loss estimates not only express likelihoods of different pay scales but also factors such as increased commuting costs and periods of not working and not obtaining UI.

Despite their hypothetical nature, the assumed conditions are being realistic, or even understated as representations of the likely labor market experiences of former LB and other affected workers, and the consequent community income loss.

REFERENCES

Annual Planning Report, Fiscal Year 1978, Utica-Rome Labor Area, June 1977.

Applicants and Openings, Utica-Rome Metropolitan Area, May 1977.

Characteristics of the Insured Unemployed, Utica-Rome Area, April-June 1977.

Duncan, Otis D. and Albert J. Reiss. *Social Characteristics of Urban and Rural Communities, 1950.* New York: Wiley, 1956.

Economic Development Administration loan application documents, June 24, 1976, mimeo.

Economic Profile, Herkimer County, New York, Fall 1975.

Employment and Earnings, U.S. Department of Labor, September 1976-September 1977.

Garnick, Daniel H. "Differential Regional Multiplier Models," *Journal of Regional Science,* 10, 1, 1970, pp. 35-47.

Grant, Eugene, W.G. Ireson, and R.S. Leavenworth. *Principles of Engineering Economy.* New York: Ronald Press Company, 1976.

Haber, William, L.A. Ferman, and J.R. Hudson. *The Impact of Technological Change.* Kalamazoo, MI: W.E. Upjohn Institute, September 1963.

Hiring Specifications, New York State, May 1977, pp. 79-91.

Holen, Arlene. *Losses to Workers Displaced by Plant Closure or Layoff: A Survey of the Literature.* Arlington, VA: Center for Naval Analyses, November 1976.

Howe, Charles W. *Benefit-Cost Analysis for Water System Planning.* Washington: American Geophysical Union, 1971.

JOBFLO: A Report on Demand Occupations, Utica-Rome, August, 1977.

Lantz, Herman R. *People of Coal Town.* Carbondale, IL: Southern Illinois University Press, Arcturus Books, 1971.

Levinson, David. "Displaced Pottery Workers' Adjustment to Layoff," in *Weathering Layoff in a Small Community*. U.S. Bureau of Labor Statistics, Bulletin No. 1516, Washington: Government Printing Office, June 1966.

Long, Richard J. "The Effect of Employee Ownership on Organization, Employee Job Attitudes and Organization Performance: A Tentative Framework and Empirical Findings," *Human Relations*, January 1978, pp. 29-48.

Lynch, John E. *Local Economic Development After Military Base Closures*. New York: Praeger, 1970.

McNulty, James E. "A Test of the Time Dimension in Economic Base Analysis," *Land Economics*, 53, 3, August 1977, pp. 359-368.

Miernyk, William H. *Inter-Industry Labor Mobility*. Boston, MA: Northeastern University, 1955.

Palmer, Edgar Z. *The Community Economic Base and Multiplier*. University of Nebraska Business Research Bulletin No. 63, 1958.

Park, Se-Hark. "A Statistical Investigation of the Urban Employment Multiplier," *Mississippi Valley Journal of Business and Economics*, 6, 1, Fall 1970, pp. 10-20.

"Preliminary Information for Proposal to Purchase Library Bureau Division of Sperry Rand Corporation." Moval Management Corporation, March 31, 1976, mimeo.

Shultz, George P. and A.R. Webster. *Strategies for the Displaced Worker*. New York: Harper and Row, 1966.

Tolles, H. Arnold. "The Post-Layoff Experience of Displaced Carpet-Mill Workers," in *Weathering Layoff in a Small Community*. U.S. Bureau of Labor Statistics Bulletin No. 1516. Washington: Government Printing Office, June 1966.

Udis, Bernard. *The Economic Consequences of Reduced Military Spending*. Lexington, MA: Lexington Books, 1973.

Utica-Rome, Labor Area Summary (formerly *Manpower Review*), January 1975-September 1978, Vol. II, No. 1-Vol. II, No. 9.

Weimer, Arthur M. and H. Hoyt. *Principles of Urban Real Estate*. New York: The Ronald Press, 1939.

Weiss, S. and E. Gooding. "Estimation of Differential Employment Multipliers In a Small Regional Economy," *Land Economics,* 44, 1968, pp. 235-244.

Whitman, Edmund S. and W.J. Schmidt. *Plant Relocation: A Case History of a Move.* New York: American Management Association, 1966.

Winpinsinger, William W. "Labor Participation on Corporate Boards," *Executive,* 33, Spring 1977, pp. 20-22.

6
Cost-Benefit Analysis: Social

Because techniques of social accounting are relatively undeveloped, the social elements of the cost-benefit analysis are particularly problematic. The difficulty is exacerbated by the insistence of administrators, policy makers, and many economic analysts that monetary values be attached to important factors in the analysis. Otherwise, determination of mental, physical, and social pathology could be measured by counting changes in the incidence of such behaviors. These issues are far less critical in the particular case of the Mohawk Valley because the economic analysis produces a ratio favorable to the CEF strategy. Had the results been ambiguous or slightly opposed to the project, the social costs and benefits would be critical. Because the CEF strategy must be examined in a variety of community contexts, the analysis proceeds on the assumption that social factors are as important to a decision on community strategy as economic ones.

SOCIAL BENEFITS

Avoided Costs

Although most benefits again fall under the rubric of avoided costs, there are some which accrue through the action of mobilizing the community to meet the shutdown crisis. The factors which are important to the analysis are both individual (psychological and physiological) and community (sociological and political) level.

A substantial number of studies have confirmed the adverse individual effects of unemployment and have focused explicitly on the issue of plant shutdown. Harvey Brenner's report, *Estimating the Social Costs of National Economic Policy: Implications for Mental and Physical Health and Criminal Aggression (1976),* commissioned by the Congressional Joint Economic Committee, is a comprehensive look at the social costs of unemployment, inflation, and per capita income. Using data covering the period from 1940 to the early 1970s, Brenner found relationships between economic changes and (1) general mortality, (2) cirrhosis of the liver, (3) suicide, (4) homicide, (5) mental hospital admissions, (6) cardiovascular and renal disease mortality, and (7) imprisonment.

Of particular interest are the relationships between these social indicators and unemployment. In one cross-sectional national analysis he found significant increases in all the measures of social pathology in relation to the 1.4 percent increase in unemployment which occurred in 1970. Table 6-1 shows the proportionate increases which appear in his regression models.

Table 6-1
Impact of a 1.4 Percent Increase in Unemployment in 1970

Social Indicator	Percent Change
General mortality	2.7
Suicide	5.7
Mental hospital admission	4.7
State prison admission	5.6
Homicide	8.0
Cirrhosis of the liver	2.7
Cardiovascular and renal failure mortality	2.7

Despite some statistical problems in projecting these national estimates to the city level, Policy and Management Associates (1978) have done so in estimating the impact of the closing of Youngstown Sheet and Tube on the Youngstown-Warren SMSA.

With a Mohawk Valley population of only 30,000, the actual change in these social indicators was likely to have been small, but nevertheless, the increased unemployment in an already depressed area would have had a real cost.

Considerable research and anecdotal evidence reconfirm Brenner's conclusions. Kasl, Cobb and Brooks' (1968) field experiment examined two groups of middle-aged men with stable work histories. One group consisting of individuals who had lost their jobs in a plant shutdown showed higher cholesterol and serum uric acid levels than those who remained employed. Members of the laid off group returned to pre-shutdown levels of blood chemistry once reemployed. Kasl and Cobb (1970) reconfirm these results in another study using blood pressure as a physiological measure and Cobb (1974) later shows that termination due to plant closing exacerbates chronic medical disorders.

Case studies provide dramatic rallying points for those who wish to show the importance of employment for mental health, but are even more useful in illustrating the linkages between employment and social relationships. Strange's (1977) in-depth interviews with 30 employees displaced by the closing of a chemical plant in a company town in Appalachia called Saltville show that the closure produced (1) increased alcohol consumption, (2) diminished appetite and weight loss, (3) ulcer development, (4) psychological withdrawal, (5) loss of self-confidence, (6) inability to adjust to new work, (7) social isolation, (8) mid-life crises, and (9) loss of sense of meaningful continuity to life.

However, Strange finds social effects beyond these individual ones. The loss of the interpersonal network provided by the shared workplace fed back onto Saltville's social structure in the form of a decreased sense of interpersonal trust and social control in the town. He argues that this occurrence is comparable to Kai Erikson's (1976) finding that a state of "collective trauma" existed in the community remaining after the Buffalo Creek flood disaster. Erikson argues that the flood resulted in "a blow to the tissues of social life that damages the bonds linking people together and impairs the prevailing sense of community" (quoted in Strange, 1977: 67). Strange saw the loss of the plant which had been the core of Saltville's existence for 75 years as a parallel form of disaster to the flood.

The steel plant layoffs in Youngstown have also been described in these terms, "Many of the victims . . . have experienced shock as severe as if they had been in a natural disaster." (Policy and Management Associates, 1978: 82). Foltman's (1968) study in Buffalo uses the vocabulary of a cataclysmic disaster and a description of the Kasanof's Bakery closing in Boston discussed the feeling of "coming home to find your house burned down" (*Boston-Phoenix Observer,* April 20, 1977).

The catastrophe is the loss of community, of social relationships and of the central activity of ordinary lives. Work has a major impact on a variety of aspects of life beside individual mental and physical health (Meissner, 1971). Obviously, stress and mental health problems affect other relationships including family, social participation, and alienation. The Youngstown impact analysis argues that:

> The inactivity and boredom which often result from unemployment can lead to such hostile behavior as wife beating and child abuse. Indeed, an increased tendency toward marital conflict is viewed as a direct consequence of extended unemployment. Furthermore, numerous studies have shown inverse relationships between socio-economic status on the one hand and divorce rates, desertions, and illegitimacy on the other (Policy and Management Associates, 1978: 83).

In an examination of the economics of early child development, Fein points out that child-rearing conditions where parents are under stress, with disruptive, unstable family life are associated with: (1) reduced levels of intellectual functioning; (2) poor school performances; (3) social aggression; and (4) intergroup conflict. She comments that "after 10 years of costly socio-educational programs we have yet to find an inexpensive, efficient reversal strategy" (1976: 45).

A second social cost of unemployment and plant shutdowns is the social disintegration which results from rapid changes such as those which Durkheim associated with industrialization and urbanization. Plant shutdowns disrupt workers' lives without permitting them the opportunity to control the economic process; they are treated as instruments of production. This form of alienation is evident in Aiken, Ferman and Sheppard's (1968) study of an auto plant shutdown. Worker attitudes of alienation and political extremism were increased by the job loss.

Finally, social withdrawal is a result of job loss. Crysdale's (1968) study of an electric plant in Canada notes the centrality of jobs to social stability and self-identity. He finds that job loss and consequent status loss result in withdrawal from secondary associations (church, clubs, etc.) and to either apathy or extremes in political behavior.

Results consistent with these were found by Pope (1964) through interviews with high seniority, older blue-collar workers and low-income white-collar workers. He showed a significant negative relationship between months unemployed or laid off and the level of formal and informal voluntary social participation. Clague, et al., also noted what they termed "the growth of anti-social attitudes" (1934: 112) subsequent to plant closure.

Community Control Benefits

These unmeasurable avoided costs are not the only benefits which emerge from the establishment of a CEF. Positive benefits occur in two ways. First, control over the local economic base is returned to the local community and common interests are created. Second, the act of mobilization to meet a community crisis creates the integration, knowledge, and organizational infrastructure needed to meet future crises.

The benefits of a close community-industry relationship were elaborated in discussions by Warner and Low (1947). The interests of industry and community coincide and mutual accommodation occurs in problem solving. With absentee control, policies are decided without local input and corporate policies often dictate reduced involvement with local banks, suppliers, and consumers. One study of this issue by Mills and Ulmer (1946) found that cities with small industries and stable employment displayed high levels of "civic spirit," educational opportunities and recreational facilities. Walton (1968) showed that control from outside the community causes more conflictual local political structures and disrupts the local norms of political and social activity.

The reintegration of industrial and social life not only increases the accountability of the firm to community interests, but also leads to the creation of collective interest itself. Jacob and Toscano's book on the integration of political communities asserts that "the essence of the integrative relationship is seen as *collective action to promote mutual interest*" (1964: 5). Kanter finds the same principle of communality in the utopian communities she studied (1972).

Reintegration and the creation of collective community interests are evident in the Mohawk Valley case. The "Save the Library Bureau" campaign was a clear episode of collective action which created common interest in the face of the potential disruption of the Sperry Rand decision to shut down rather than sell the plant. Community accountability is evident in the controversy over the decision to purchase the steel shelving plant outside the Valley and subsequent decisions to increase local employment as business expands. Further, common ownership led the workforce and management to meet a one month slack period caused by the initial announced closing with an "across the board" four-day work week rather than layoffs by seniority. The seven member board of directors contains four outsiders, two of whom are community business representatives, and one an economic development officer. The Library Bureau is the topic of much interest in the Mohawk Valley and its operations are followed through community newspapers, "bar room discussion," and dinner table conversation.

The second major benefit of the community mobilization to purchase the plant and community concern over its fate is of longer term and perhaps more significant consequence. The community has acted in a manner which counters the contemporary trend toward absentee control of local economies and the resultant incapacity to deal with community crises.

When Warren (1963) and others described the changes in American community structure which occurred since the beginning of the 20th century, they described the vertical integration of communities into the overall system of economic production. Communities became linked into a system of interdependent relationships which were largely controlled by elements outside the community. These vertical linkages affected the relationships between elements within communities which were termed horizontal linkages. Community groups, local governments, and individuals became dependent upon community members whose allegiance lay outside the community. Dependence upon absentee controlled corporations destroyed the locally committed populations' ability to act on its own. The weakening of horizontal linkages in communities is analogous to the trained incapacity of some bureaucrats (Merton, 1968). When a new situation arises in which the extra local interests are either removed or disinterested, the local population cannot act. It has lost the infrastructure of organizations and skills which are needed to meet current needs. Walton (1968) hypothesized that greater vertical ties imply a smaller scope for local power groups and that coordinated community action is more difficult.

Thus, Warren defines community development as "a deliberate and sustained attempt to strengthen the horizontal pattern of the community" and quotes Sanders' description of this development process as

> change from a condition where one or two people or a small elite within or without the local community make a decision for the rest of the people to a condition where the people themselves make these decisions about matters of common concern; from a state of minimum to maximum cooperation; from a condition where few participate to one where many participate; from a condition where all resources and specialists come from outside to one where local people make the most use of their own resources (Warren, 1963: 324).

Federal government policy which encourages the establishment of local economic development agencies partially develops local organizational capacity to act, but development agencies do not particularly emphasize locally controlled business. A community based effort toward community-employee ownership creates a different type of organizational development and capacity from that based on a development agency alone.

The events which occurred in the purchase of the Library Bureau are an instance of Warren's community development. The community pooled its resources to achieve a result not possible through reliance upon outsiders. The community learning which took place through the change in ownership represents an increase in knowledge which is as important a part of economic development as creating an industrial park might be and is more important than having found another absentee buyer would have been.

When the Standard Desk Company closed several years earlier, the community had not had the capacity to act. In the Library Bureau case, the organizational capacity of the community was increased and knowledge of the mechanisms for obtaining government assistance was developed. Not only were the local economic development district and county area development agency offices in place, but there was a businessmen's assistance committee and a management consulting firm which studied the economic viability of the company and developed a financing plan. Local entrepreneurial talent, which has been crucial to employee ownership efforts, was committed to the project (Stern and Hammer, 1978). The development district office supplied knowledge and resources for obtaining federal assistance and the business assistance committee raised funds for campaign costs. The business leaders developed a fund raising plan similar to that used in a United Fund drive. The plan depended on the existence of organized groups in the community which could be mobilized for commitments of time and capital. In short, the organizational infrastructure of the community permitted the newly created organization, the Mohawk Valley Community Corporation, to raise the capital required for the plant purchase.

The importance of community organizational capacity and the ability to mobilize resources is critical. It is the same capacity which is at the basis of social movements (McCarthy and Zald, 1977) and revolutions (Oberschall, 1973). It is analogous to the organization which emerges in community disasters. The community both used its existing organizations and created new ones to accomplish the local purchase, and the mobilization experience has left critical residues. First there is the increased organizational capacity of the community; second, the local population developed confidence in local leaders and the ability of the community to meet local crises; third, knowledge and skills for utilizing available government resources merged from the experience.

Figure 6-1 pictures the model of community response to crisis through organizational capacity. The result of the increased organizational capacity and mobilization skills of the community is its lessened vulnerability to decisions made primarily through means and according to criteria which can be crucially different from its own. The community-employee ownership of a vital segment of the local economic base and the action of obtaining that ownership, gives the community greater ability to deal with fluctuations in economic activity in the larger society. The local population is committed to continuity of local employment and it has developed the skills needed to help itself. While the community is still subject to the economic pressures of the market, the increase in community autonomy and economic security is a clear benefit of the CEF strategy.

We initially suggested that increased worker participation in firm decision making was an additional benefit, particularly in light of evidence provided by studies in the U.S. (Conte and Tannenbaum, 1977), Israel (Melman, 1975), and Chile (Espinosa and Zimbalist, 1978). Participation presumably affects not only production but also spills over to political and social activities (Pateman, 1970).

However, the potential benefit of having a more participatory firm is another factor in which the theoretical possibilities associated with a CEF need to be differentiated from the case

168

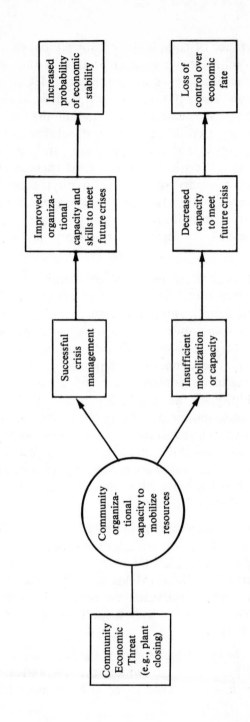

Figure 6-1
Managing Community Economic Crisis

being studied. The MVCC has retained a basically conventional day-to-day decision making process, although a higher degree of consultation, especially with the two union presidents, does occur. The integrative collective action to promote mutual interests found so beneficial in the community during the acquisition campaign has not been continued into the everyday activity of the firm. This situation is not surprising, and a number of possible explanations exist. For a start, despite the change in the formal structure of the organization, patterns of behavior and attitudes learned under the previous structure tend to persist even after a change. Usual behavior and attitudes were to an extent put aside during the crisis atmosphere of the acquisition, but since then "business as usual" has generally prevailed. Whether other reasons exist beyond custom and whether this situation is preferable, are separate issues from the decision to purchase the firm.

William F. Whyte's examination of this and similar cases leads him to suggest that the apparent contradiction between ownership and decision making power will be transitory (1978). The local unions of the firm have begun to discuss the disparity between their ownership rights and actual influence within the firm. Over the five-year period assumed in the evaluation, the community may yet be able to count increased employee participation in everyday decision making as a benefit. However, the uncertainty of this participation is such as to greatly discount its possibility as a benefit in this analysis.

Social Costs

The establishment of the CEF means that the economic base of the community changed ownership, but otherwise remained the same as before the threatened closing. So long as the community has not invested its resources in an enterprise which is irrevocably headed for economic failure, social costs are very speculative if they actually exist at all.

One possibility is that the community drew heavily on a limited supply of political influence, which may be unavailable at some period in the future. The workers and residents appealed to all local politicians, their U.S. senators, and the governor. One U.S. senator in particular had to use considerable pressure to obtain Sperry Rand's cooperation in the change of ownership. Such actions are not without cost. For the community, the use of its influence for the CEF may hinder obtaining a future objective, or a political debt may have to be repaid.

Although the theoretical discussion suggests the possible integrating effects of a CEF, there may actually be more conflict in the community. Previously, the community, especially most of those working in the plant, were united against a common external enemy. Deficiencies regarding the operation and conditions in the plant and its treatment of the community could previously be blamed on Sperry Rand. Now that the community is itself responsible, it has more areas for dispute and divisiveness, in a much less well-defined situation. Both management and workers, and the firm and the community now have more reason for interaction, and this alone may lead to conflicts (Coser, 1956). As Coser emphasizes, the conflict may have beneficial functions, but it is worth noting as a possible cost to the community.

The possibility of conflict may be exacerbated by various expectations having been raised through the change of ownership which, if not fulfilled, can lead to greater dissatisfaction than exists in more conventional firms. The whole situation may result in stress because of readjustment problems, a less defined situation, more responsibility, and increased group pressure to perform. As noted earlier, stress can have negative psychological and psychophysiological effects.

At the present time, however, these speculative costs seem outweighed by the community and individual benefits of having maintained the Library Bureau and placed it under local ownership.

REFERENCES

Aiken, Michael, L.A. Ferman, and H.L. Sheppard. *Economic Failure, Alienation and Extremism.* Ann Arbor, MI: University of Michigan Press, 1968.

Husock, Howard. *Boston-Phoenix Observer,* April 20, 1977.

Brenner, M. Harvey. "Estimating the Social Costs of National Economic Policy: Implications for Mental and Physical Health and Criminal Aggression," in *Anchoring the Goals of the Employment Act of 1946-30th Anniversary Review,* Vol. 1, paper No. 5, Washington: Government Printing Office, 1976.

Clague, Ewan, W.J. Couper, and E.W. Bakke. *After the Shutdown.* New Haven, CT: Yale University, 1934.

Cobb, Sidney. "Physiologic Changes in Men Whose Jobs Were Abolished," *Journal of Psychosomatic Research,* 18, 1974, pp. 245-258.

Conte, M. and A.S. Tannenbaum. *Employee Ownership.* Report to the Economic Development Administration. Ann Arbor, MI: Survey Research Center, 1978.

Coser, Lewis. *The Functions of Social Conflict.* Glencoe, IL: Free Press, 1956.

Crysdale, Stewart. *Problems of Employment and Relocation of the Workforce.* Toronto, United Steel Workers, 1968.

Espinosa, Juan and Andrew S. Zimbalist. *Economic Democracy.* New York: Academic Press, 1978.

Erikson, Kai T. *Everything In Its Path. Destruction of Community in the Buffalo Creek Flood.* New York: Simon and Schuster, 1976.

Fein, Greta G. "Hidden Costs: Some Speculations on the Economics of Early Development." The Merrill-Palmer Institute, June 1976, pp. 42-50.

Foltman, Felician F. *White- and Blue-Collar in a Mill Shutdown:* A Case *Study in Relative Redundancy.* Ithaca, NY: New York State School of Industrial and Labor Relations, paperback No. 6, 1968.

Jacob, Phillip E. and J.U. Toscano. *The Integration of Political Communities.* Philadelphia, PA: J.B. Lippincott, 1964.

Kanter, Rosabeth. *Commitment and Community.* Cambridge, MA: Harvard University Press, 1972.

Kasl, Stanislav and Sidney Cobb. "Blood Pressure Changes in Men Undergoing Job Loss," *Psychosomatic Medicine,* 62, January/February 1970, pp. 19-38.

Kasl, Stanislav, Sidney Cobb, and G.W. Brooks. "Changes in Serum Uric Acid and Cholesterol Levels in Men Undergoing Job Loss," *Journal of the American Medical Association,* CCVI, November 1968, pp. 1500-1507.

McCarthy, John and Mayer Zald. "Resource Mobilization and Social Movements: A Partial Theory," *American Journal of Sociology,* 82, May 1977, pp. 1212-1242.

Meissner, Martin. "The Long Arm of the Job," *Industrial Relations,* 10, 1971, pp. 239-260.

Melman, Seymour. "Industrial Efficiency Under Managerial Versus Cooperative Decision-Making." In *Self-Governing Socialism,* 2. Branko Horvat, M. Markovic, and R. Supek, eds. White Plains, NY: International Arts and Sciences Press, Inc., 1975, pp. 203-220.

Merton, Robert K. *Social Theory and Social Structure.* New York: The Free Press, 1968.

Mills, C. Wright and M. Ulmer. Small Business and Civic Welfare: Report on the Smaller War Plants Corporation to the Special Committee to Study Problems of American Small Business. Senate Document No. 135, 79th Congress, 2nd Session, Washington, DC, 1946, Serial No. 11036.

Oberschall, Anthony. *Social Conflict and Social Movements.* Englewood Cliffs, NJ: Prentice-Hall, Inc., 1973.

Pateman, Carole. *Participation and Democratic Theory.* London, England: Cambridge University Press, 1970.

Policy and Management Associates, Inc. "Socioeconomic Costs and Benefits of the Community-Worker Ownership Plan to the Youngstown-Warren SMSA," Report for the National Center of Economic Alternatives, Washington: April 1978.

Pope, Hallowell. "Economic Deprivation and Social Participation in a Group of 'Middle Class' Factory Workers," *Social Problems,* 11, Winter 1964, pp. 290-300.

Stern, Robert N. and Tove Helland Hammer. "Buying Your Job: Factors Affecting the Success or Failure of Employee Acquisition Attempts," *Human Relations,* 31, 12, 1978, pp. 1101-1117.

Strange, Walter G. "Job Loss: A Psychosocial Study of Worker Reactions to a Plant Closing in a Company Town in Southern Appalachia." Ph.D. dissertation, Cornell University, 1977.

Walton, John. "The Vertical Axis of Community Organization and the Structure of Power," *Social Science Quarterly,* 48, December 1968, pp. 353-368.

Warner, W. Lloyd and J.O. Low. *The Social System of the Modern Factory.* New Haven, CT: Yale University Press, 1947.

Warren, Roland. *The Community in America.* Chicago: Rand-McNally Company, 1963.

Whyte, William F. "In Support of Voluntary Employee Ownership," *Society,* 15, 6, September/October 1978, pp. 73-82.

7
System Level Analysis

This cost-benefit analysis began by violating the common practice of examining costs and benefits from an economy wide point of view. Often such a view presents an analysis from the perspective of governmental agencies designed to assist specific projects or from the relative costs and benefits to some mythical taxpayer. The community level analysis certainly shows that the CEF strategy was reasonable from the perspective of the towns in the Mohawk Valley, but the purchase required two million dollars in loans from the Economic Development Administration. Is the benefit to the community a cost to the federal government or is it an investment which in turn provides the benefits of community survival, tax flows, and a stronger economy?

Alternative Strategies for Government
Assistance in Plant Closures

The federal outlay must be evaluated in terms of alternative uses for these funds. The question is not one of broad social priorities such as the trade-off between investing in community jobs and producing an additional piece of military equipment. Rather, the issue is the availability of alternative uses of government funds aimed at job creation or job stability.

An evaluation study is obliged to compare all feasible alternatives, but this study has basically evaluated only one alternative: retaining the plant through community-employee ownership. There were no other means of continuing the firm and the comparisons were made with the likely consequences of a closure in mind. However, there are approaches to dealing with plant shutdowns and shutdown-related unemployment which provide alternatives to the CEF strategy for retaining the plant.

An ideal evaluation would compare the CEF to all feasible community and societal approaches to closures, using commensurable criteria. Though the CEF has a favorable benefit-cost ratio in this case, other alternatives may provide equally attractive ratios. Unfortunately the magnitude and difficulties of a full comparative evaluation are enormous. The most significant obstacle is obtaining commensurate measures of results for the large number of disparate existing programs. Though comparisons may assist in setting priorities for resource allocation, judgment is complicated by the complementarity of many of the programs; they are seldom completely alternatives.

However, a broad-gauge, qualitative evaluation of relevant alternatives is possible. Strategies focus upon either the demand or the supply side of the labor market. Job demand, or job creation, programs meet plant closures and unemployment through local booster groups, tax incentives, the Economic Development Administration (EDA) programs, public service employment, and influences upon aggregate demand. A job supply strategy suggests the provision of retraining, relocation assistance, and information to facilitate workers' transfer to new areas or occupations when plant shutdowns occur.

Comparison between the CEF strategy and several of these alternatives has been implied in the discussion of the continued structural unemployment of economically depressed areas. Many of the alternatives fail to deal with structural unemployment problems. The CEF strategy does not solve all the difficulties inherent in the alternatives and is not necessarily superior to them, but it is sufficiently beneficial to merit inclusion in the arsenal of measures available to counter some cases of community economic decline. The available alternatives to accepting plant shutdowns suggest policy changes which would aid communities faced with the prospect of lost jobs.

Federal Loans and Grants

Community-employee ownership is a strategy aimed at the demand side of the labor market. This particular case and those of South Bend, Lathe, and Okonite, have relied upon the Economic Development Administration (EDA) in order to obtain capital. The agency generally concentrates on obtaining new employment opportunities through infrastructural or company-level aid.

One evaluation of EDA charges that much project selection is politically motivated; detrimental plant relocations are often encouraged, project selection guidelines are unclear, and, the incidence of poor projects is above an acceptable level. The authors of that evaluation claim that often EDA provides much benefit for upper middle-class businessmen and local governments rather than the unemployed or those with low income. In short, "the $2.5 billion the agency has expended has had little impact on the unemployment problem of the country" (Kovarik and Devolites, 1977: 9). Of most significance, however, is the finding that EDA's national office only keeps records on approved applications. Thus, no comparison with alternative uses of the funds is possible and the opportunity cost of any given loan is effectively zero. Comparison between alternative projects is not made formally. One possible interpretation is that funds allocated on a regional basis are distributed with some principle of equity in mind. On the other hand, Kovarik and Devolites provide data which suggests that political influence is a significant facilitator of loan funding.

Pressman and Wildavsky in *Implementation* (1973), give a comprehensive description of a disappointing EDA project. Briefly, private businesses obtained capital on the promise of providing minority employment, in Oakland, California, but did not fulfill the commitments. The project became enmeshed in unsuccessful attempts to enforce the promises through bureaucratic means after the capital was already distributed.

The EDA has generally worked to lower unemployment through the relatively indirect means of promoting the preconditions for business development. This approach can go awry because the interests of the businesses are not necessarily congruent with those of the unemployed and the declining communities. When common interests do not exist, it is difficult to force the desired development through bureaucratic means. Where a firm is community-employee owned, the EDA's aid may be more effective because the target population presumably has more control over its use. A CEF is accountable and has interests more directly compatible with economic development.

Federal policies have often been criticized because the intended recipients do not always obtain the benefits intended for them since they do not control the process of resource use and distribution. Moguloff (1970) reviewed federal policies and practices regarding citizen participation[1] and found that, although many programs noted its desirability, there was little citizen participation in practice. Piven and Cloward's (1971) critique of programs for the poor focused upon the lack of organizational capacity and skills among those who were supposed to benefit and a resultant inability to benefit from the funds made available under federal welfare programs. CEFs should be able to improve target populations' control over some economic development programs. The stake and commitment provided by ownership and higher knowledge levels (through daily employee involvement and stockholder informational requirements) will better ensure the desired implementation and outcome levels.

Faux (1971) points to the case of the Department of Labor in 1967-68 providing $5 million to firms promising to locate in the East Los Angeles barrio and hire 1,500 local residents. After the scheme failed, the federal government report stated that the basic defect was that the community had no control over it. Similar critiques have been made of Small Business Administration and Farmers Home Administration programs.

---

1. Participation is defined by Moguloff as "an act or a series of acts by which the 'citizen' has the opportunity to influence the distribution of benefits or losses which may be visited upon him (or upon those people he represents) as a result of Federally supported activity" (p. 2).

Locational Incentives

A major strategy of job creation has been the offering of tax incentives or loan guarantees for locating a plant in a particular community or state. Some cost-benefit analyses of these incentives find that when a new firm locates in an area, the economic payoff outweighs the cost in taxes to the community. Marginal businesses may be able to survive a short time longer with tax relief, but a business which is economically unviable will not be helped much.

There are two flaws in the cost-benefit assessment of tax incentives. The first is the assumption that state and local taxes are important in locational decisions. Studies suggest that labor, raw material, and market play a much larger role than taxes in determining company location. Taxes are seldom more than 1 or 2 percent of total costs (Harrison, 1974) and are given far more publicity than their business reality warrants (Schmenner, 1975). Similarly, Stillwell (1978) reports on an Ohio study of 98 companies closing down plants just as the state instituted a series of locational tax breaks. Only three companies indicated that Ohio tax policies were a factor in their relocation decisions. Tax incentives appear to work in creating jobs in a very limited number of cases. Similarly, industrial parks may go unoccupied or underutilized, becoming a drain on local resources rather than a mechanism of growth. Haber, Ferman and Hudson's (1963) review of plant shutdown studies found local booster campaigns relatively ineffective. Bearse, examining economic planning in New Jersey argued that

> it is very unlikely that in any given year the major investment decisions of more than a very few firms would be influenced by the availability of subsidized loans. Nevertheless, a large number of firms take advantage of such loans. The opportunity costs of current programs may therefore be very high (1977: 191).

Stillwell quotes the Cleveland Growth Association, an industry group which formerly pushed for tax abatements, as saying that "tax abatement is not an incentive to prevent a relocation from

Ohio to Alabama or Texas. . . . Taxes probably would not play a major role" (1978: 46).

However, tax incentive plans and booster programs continue to be popular and suggest a second flaw in the locational incentive strategy. Everyone is trying to use it. Thus, local and state governments believe that they will lose industry and weaken their economic bases if they do not offer incentives. The result is what some call a "pure give away" (Bearse, 1977: 25) as corporations push for tax breaks or locally financed infrastructure such as industrial parks. One byproduct is that the tax breaks for new industry place the burden of local tax support on older plants (Sheridan, 1977) and communities and states have a harder time paying for the services they must provide. The 70 Ohio school districts on the brink of financial insolvency are a partial testimony to the problem (Stillwell, 1978). In the case of Sperry's Univac plant which closed in Utica the year before the threatened closing in Herkimer, a generous proposal of tax relief and free land was insufficient to alter the corporate decision. For some communities, the tax incentive is believed to have worked, but overall, results of this approach are minimal if not actually negative. Though a community may wish to institute an overall program of incentives, CEFs are unlikely to require them given that community members own the company.

Public Service Employment

The federal government has been involved in two particular job creation efforts which receive public attention. The Employment Tax Credit program provides incentives for employers to create new jobs and has cost approximately $2.5 billion per year. Unfortunately, the assessment of this program in President Carter's urban policy statement is that there has been little impact on hiring decisions. *The Wall Street Journal* reported on August 11, 1976 that not even the 7 billion dollar a year investment tax credit had succeeded in creating new jobs.

The other major attempt at job creation—public service employment (PSE)—has also been severely criticized. The program obviously has great impact; the number of persons employed under it nearly doubled from fiscal years 1977 to 1979, reaching 750,000 with an expenditure of $12 billion. But, Carter has criticized it as short-run and regards economic development as the long term answer. A General Accounting Office evaluation of Department of Labor PSE programs for 1974-1976 included criticisms that: (1) relatively few participants obtained permanent unsubsidized jobs; (2) the programs were sometimes not used to create new job opportunities; (3) ineligible participants got into the program (Comptroller General, 1977).

Local boards or Community Development Corporation (CDC) types of organizations should have more control over PSE. Similarly, CEFs may be a useful vehicle for PSE because they would combine local accountability and responsiveness with providing capital equipment complementary to the PSE; "makework" ought to be minimized.

Some long-run anti-unemployment proposals are parallel in many respects to CEF forms of development. One example is the recently established Massachusetts Community Development Finance Corporation (CDFC). The CDFC will act as a private venture capitalist, but will provide equity and debt financing only to ventures controlled by community development corporations in depressed areas. Canada has made similar initiatives, such as the Local Employment Assistance Program, begun in 1972, which funds CDC-type development.

CDCs have been enthusiastically hailed by some observers since their earliest development (Faux, 1971). More recent authors have extensively elaborated their economic and political potential advantages (Goldrich, 1978). Although evaluations have shown mixed outcomes, they can be adequately summarized as indicating that "the positive results attained by some show that the concept can work" (Subcommittee of the Committee on Government Operations, 1977: 23). The performance of CDCs has been marred by poor management and low capitalization in CDC business ventures, and less than desired local area participation and interest in some CDCs. These problems may be lessened by CDCs conforming more to CEFs, because of the possible motivational, productivity, resource-pooling, and stake-producing advantages discussed earlier.

The federal government has also attempted to influence job supply by adjusting aggregate demand in the economy. However, monetary and fiscal policies have been inadequate to remove unemployment in important age, sex, race, occupational, and regional subgroups, given inflation and other constraints. Such policies certainly have not altered the plant shutdown problem. More specific local solutions are required.

Labor Supply

Approaches to unemployment and shutdowns which stress the supply side of the labor market usually include training and retraining programs. The evaluation and comparison of these programs is very difficult because studies have often ignored secondary employment effects of displacement. Plant closure studies show the overwhelming importance of labor market demand in determining reemployment rates. Training is little use if jobs are not available.

There are more fundamental objections to anti-unemployment approaches which work on the supply side, particularly regarding shutdown-related unemployment. Advocates of training and relocation assistance, believe that societal welfare is increased by higher geographic labor mobility. While there are undoubtedly benefits gained from geographic mobility, these are difficult and costly to obtain and conventional conclusions regarding the desirability of labor mobility are based upon narrow economic and individual level criteria alone. These types of arguments, elaborated earlier, suggest the need for demand side approaches such as those represented by CDCs and community-employee ownership.

Income maintenance experiments, social services, unemployment insurance and specialized aid such as the Trade Readjustment Assistance Act are designed to ease the unemployment problem but do not address the fundamental question of how to maintain employment and give individuals some control over their own fate. All else being equal, there should be a preference for allocating resources to a productive activity such as a CEF.

Trade unions in this country generally provide little help for shutdown-related problems. Mick's review of contract provisions for bargaining units with at least 10,000 employees shows that "at best only one-fourth of organized labor appears to be covered by any provision related to plant movement" (1975: 207). Even the protection which does exist is post hoc, not preventative—the most common provision is interplant transfer. Most of the other three-quarters of the U.S. workforce which is not unionized is likely to have, at best, no more protection.

POLICY CONSIDERATIONS

These issues have attracted considerable attention including policy suggestions and initiatives in Congress. Policy considerations related to this study fall into two categories: those which address the plant shutdown problem and those aimed at facilitating employee or community-employee ownership.

Plant Shutdown Proposals

In the summer of 1978, representatives of the United Automobile Workers, United Steel Workers, and International Association of Machinists made a study tour of Europe to examine the policies and practices of other industrialized countries regarding plant shutdowns. They found that nearly all European countries provided greater protection for workers than the U.S. does and in particular, noted requirements for advanced notice regarding shutdowns and severance pay. They were particularly impressed with Sweden's investment in government approved projects designed to smooth the distribution of economic production geographically and were encouraged by the planning systems of large corporations which drafted and updated five-year development plans and provided greater control over the level of job opportunities. A set of policy recommendations for labor and government has been produced (May, 1979).

Within the United States, the Conference on Alternative State and Local Public Policies, the Ohio Public Interest Campaign, the National Commission on Neighborhoods, and a number of other groups have carried out studies of community level economic development problems.

1. In general, these assessments agree that *corporate relocations and closings should be regulated.* These regulations should include *mandatory notice to the government, unions, workers, and the community* of the intention to close a plant. Wisconsin currently requires 60 days notice, but this period appears to be inadequate for individual community or government action. Some groups, such as the Ohio Public Interest Campaign, advocate two years advanced notice (Kelly, 1977). *Compensation to displaced workers* including transfer rights, retraining, and maintenance of health insurance should be guaranteed. The community costs should become costs to the corporation as well. A proposed Ohio law would have the corporation pay an amount equal to 10 percent of its annual wage bill into a state redevelopment fund. *Other proposals suggest lump sum payments to affected communities.* These proposals would partially convert the externalities which corporations have left to the public into internal costs to be borne by the corporation wishing to move. Labor unions should begin to negotiate such payments through collective bargaining if general legal changes are unlikely.

2. *Tax laws must be modified.* U.S. plant shutdowns are encouraged by several current tax regulations. Changes in the Trade Act of 1974 reduced tariffs on goods produced in some developing countries. The result has been both a competitive advantage for foreign goods, and more critically, an incentive for U.S. corporations to move to countries such as South Korea, Taiwan, and Mexico. Second, the ability of multinationals to defer tax payments until earnings are returned to the U.S. has further encouraged the flight of multinationals, and payments of taxes to foreign governments are usually directly deductible from

taxes owed in the U.S. The third and perhaps most important domestic issue is the ability of a company to charge the loss of a closed plant against profits in calculating taxes, then deduct the cost of building a new plant as a business expense. Such a tax provision does encourage new investment but with the current imbalance in regional energy and labor advantages it also encourages the abandonment of plants in one region for growth in another area. Stillwell (1978) points out that these tax laws have contributed to a reduction in the proportion of federal revenue contributed by corporations from about 25 percent in the late 1940s to 15 percent today. These laws encourage the abandonment of plants rather than the reinvestment and rebuilding of existing facilities.

3. *Regional differences should be minimized.* Industrial development in the U.S. is currently practiced as an entrepreneurial game. Each state and community attempts to show that it has the best business climate. In addition to the tax incentives discussed above, states and cities compete for the distinction of having the weakest labor unions or the greatest tolerance of environmental pollution (Kelly, 1977). Analysts suggest that priorities must be set first. If interstate competition is to continue then little can be done, though a Multistate Tax Commission has been formed to assure that corporations with multistate facilities do not transfer profits from high tax states to those with lower tax rates. However, should the economic development goal be a national one with fewer regional fluctuations, several changes seem critical. States should agree to "no-raiding" pacts under which advertising directly criticizing neighboring state policies and business climate would be removed. One possibility recommended by the union research team is the institution of federal taxes to offset differential tax breaks provided by state and local governments. Finally, a variety of analysts have suggested that some of the migration to the "sun belt" would be stemmed by the repeal of Taft-Hartley section 14B, though labor attempts at producing this change have failed repeatedly.

4. *Merger, takeover, and bankruptcy rules bear reexamination.* This study argues that the merger and operations policies of

conglomerate corporations are at least partially responsible for some unnecessary plant shutdowns. A number of analysts suggest that the Federal Trade Commission consider the unemployment and job loss impacts of corporate mergers. Further, small to medium-sized firms which commonly have community ties are disappearing in the current wave of conglomerate acquisitions. Takeover legislation is needed to provide the corporation being sought an opportunity to consider the purchaser's bid, and obtain information on the company's plans for the target. The critical feature must be disclosure of plans for liquidation, or continued operation.

Finally, bankruptcy law administration has provided little concern for the protection of either the workers or communities affected by a bankruptcy closure. A wider vision of the responsibility of bankruptcy courts is needed. Some proposals have also suggested change in the administrative policies of state regulators in determining the distribution of bank charters, branches, and relocation requests. The availability of capital, particularly in the case of local efforts to maintain threatened plants is critical. When capital is concentrated in urban centers, distant from the community in which it is needed, banks are hesitant to invest and may in fact miss opportunities for profitable loans. This situation is illustrated by Katz, Myerson and Strahs (1978) who describe efforts to save the Colonial Press in Clinton, Massachusetts through negotiations with banks headquartered in Worcester, Massachusetts.

5. A variety of proposals were elaborated by policy consultants Smith and McGuigan in a report on "The Public Policy Implications of Plant Closings and Runaways." They add to the above array by elaboration of the suggestions made by public interest groups, but seem to place greater emphasis on targeted federal procurement as a mechanism for preserving industry in declining areas. Such a program would provide a market for firms which might otherwise fail and is particularly important for firms whose output may be critical during military emergencies.

Community-Employee Ownership

The public interest and union groups have also recommended changes which would encourage employee or community-employee owned firms, but the recommendations have been quite tentative. Unions are concerned with the ambiguous role they would play negotiating on behalf of members who are also owners and the trade union movement has a history of distrust of cooperatives. The Ohio Public Interest Campaign recommends community-employee ownership, but warns of problems with trying to save obsolete plants, losing markets which existed because of integration into a larger company and long term capital shortages. The hesitance seems to stem from both lack of experience with CEFs resulting in uncertainty about how they work and lack of information about them. However, Michigan recently enacted a law which provides technical assistance to groups seeking to establish employee ownership to counter plant closings.

This study has not addressed itself to the internal functioning of these firms but a variety of literature is emerging which addresses such questions (Long, 1978a, 1978b; Hammer and Stern, 1979; Bernstein, 1976; Perry, 1978). Instead, the aim of this evaluation is understanding the merits of community members investing in a local corporation particularly as a mechanism for preserving the jobs based in that plant. The possibility that production lost due to the closing of a plant in one location will be picked up by production in another location is given little weight. The issue is community survival. Legislation regarding plant shutdowns is currently pending in 11 states (in addition to Michigan's law). Two pieces of federal legislation are particularly important with regard to local efforts.

1. *The Voluntary Job Preservation and Community Stabilization Act* is designed to provide direct loans and technical assistance to community-employee groups attempting to purchase plants threatened by closure. Though the legislation does not require corporations to provide early warning of intended closings, it does provide two crucial resources which communities require in order to attempt to purchase threatened plants. First,

funds and technical assistance would be available for the completion of feasibility studies to determine the prospects for financial success of the firm and capital requirements. Second, capital required for the purchase could be loaned to local groups under the proposed program. Capital has been the critical missing ingredient in a number of attempted purchases. Banks have been hesitant to risk loans to enterprises which large conglomerates have judged to be unprofitable or to take a chance on workers attempting to run their own company. Such problems are discussed more thoroughly in chapter 8, but the question of available venture capital is critical.

By March 1979, hearings on this bill had been held in the House of Representatives and companion proposals were beginning to appear in the Senate. One such proposal would incorporate early warning of planned closures and severance pay into the bill. Some support has been forthcoming from the White House which is considering incorporating provisions of the original bill into the Economic Development Administration reauthorization legislation.

2. A second important piece of legislation is the *Small Business Employee Ownership Act* which has been introduced in the Senate with bi-partisan support. It is designed to force the Small Business Administration to make loans to employee owned firms and to accept employee stock ownership trusts as qualified for loans or loan guarantees. The support of Russell Long has propelled this bill toward passage and he has given it his support because of his belief in Employee Stock Ownership Plans (ESOPs). Such plans are becoming increasingly popular as vehicles for financing corporations, providing fringe benefits to employees, and minimizing taxes (Stern and Comstock, 1978). Though a community-employee owned firm might have such a plan, as the Library Bureau does, it is a mechanism for distributing stock to employees rather than other community members. If this bill and its companion in the House should pass, additional capital for the operation of CEFs would become available.

Changes must occur at levels other than federal legislation in order to encourage successful use of the CEF strategy. Dialogue must be opened with labor union leaders on the implications of employee ownership. Though union leaders have not yet publicly opposed the Voluntary Job Preservation Act, they have considered doing so and are not yet supportive. Much of their ambivalence will be resolved as more unions actually participate in employee owned firms, but until that time questions of the role of collective bargaining, protection of union scale wages, and the viability of such firms prevent strong union support. Unions have supported efforts toward the establishment of employee owned firms only when all other alternatives were exhausted and locals have often had to insist, against international headquarters hesitance, that employee ownership was the only way to save jobs.

General beliefs in the legitimacy of employee ownership could also tolerate some improvement. Though some individuals see socialism or "un-American activity" in workers taking over plants, the reality is anything other than an illegal "takeover." Community-employee ownership of firms through stock purchase is simply the spreading of a conventional form of property ownership to a wider class of individuals. Popular belief on this subject underscores the importance of personal values in the establishment of CEFs. This study has taken the position that local community autonomy and fate control is a positively valued outcome. The data suggest that at least in the short-run, the establishment of a CEF may be an economically and socially reasonable solution.

REFERENCES

Bearse, Peter J. "Government as Innovator: A New Paradigm for State Economic Policy," in *New York State's Economic Crisis: Jobs, Income and Economic Growth*. Felician F. Foltman and P.D. McClelland, eds. Ithaca, NY: Cornell University, 1977, pp. 181-206.

Bernstein, Paul. *Workplace Demoralization: Its Internal Dynamics*. Kent, OH: Kent State University, 1976.

Comptroller General. Report to the Congress. More Benefits To Jobless Can Be Attained In Public Source Employment. Washington: Government Accounting Office, 1977.

Faux, Geoffrey. "Politics and Bureaucracy in Community Controlled Economic Development," in *Law and Contemporary Problems*. Duke University, School of Law, Spring 1971. Excerpted in Center for Community Economic Development's *Community Economics*, May 1971.

Goldrich, Daniel. "Self Management, Community Economic Control and Development and Environmental Reconstruction," paper presented to the section on "Political Conditions for Generalized Self-Management," World Congress of Sociology, Uppsala, Sweden, August 14-19, 1978.

Government Operations, Hearings Before a Subcommittee. "Operations of the Community Sources Administration." Washington: Government Printing Office, 1977.

Haber, William, L.A. Ferman, and J.R. Hudson. *Impact of Technological Change*. Kalamazoo, MI: W.E. Upjohn Institute, September 1963.

Hammer, Tove Helland and Robert N. Stern. "Employee Ownership: Implications for the Organizational Distribution of Power." Unpublished paper, Cornell University, 1979.

Harrison, Bennett. *The Economic Development of Massachusetts*. Boston: Commonwealth of Massachusetts, 1974.

Katz, Carol, Jeanne Myerson, and Stephen Strahs. "The Policy Implications of Plant Closings in Massachusetts." Manuscript, Harvard University, Cambridge, MA, 1978.

Kelly, Edward. *Industrial Exodus: Public Strategies For Control of Runaway Plants.* Washington: Conference/Alternative State and Local Public Policies, October 1977.

Kovarik and Devolites. *Employee Stock Ownership Plans and the Economic Development Administration.* Washington: National Suggestion Box, November 1, 1977.

Labor Union Study Tour. "Economic Dislocation: Plant Closings, Plant Relocations and Plant Conversion," May 1979.

Long, Richard J. "The Effect of Employee Ownership on Organization, Employee Job Attitudes and Organization Performance: A Tentative Framework and Empirical Findings," *Human Relations,* January 1978, pp. 29-48.

Long, Richard J. "The Relative Effects of Share Ownership vs. Control on Job Attitudes in an Employee-Owned Company," *Human Relations,* 31, September 1978, pp. 753-763.

Mick, Stephen S. "Social and Personal Costs of Plant Shutdowns," *Industrial Relations,* 14, 2, May 1975, pp. 203-208.

Moguloff, Melvin B. *Citizen Participation: A Review and Commentary on Federal Policies and Practices.* Washington: The Urban Institute, 1970.

Perry, Stewart. *The Scavengers.* Berkeley, CA: University of California Press, 1978.

Piven, Frances Fox and Richard A. Cloward. *Regulating the Poor.* New York: Vintage Press, 1971.

Pressman, Jeffrey L. and A.B. Wildavsky. *Implementation.* Berkeley, CA: University of California Press, 1973.

Schmenner, Roger. "City Taxes and Industry Location." Cambridge, MA: Graduate School of Business Administration, Harvard University, 1975.

Sheridan, Jon H. "Do States Neglect Old Plants for New?" *Industry Week,* July 4, 1977, pp. 43-49.

Stern, Robert N. and Phillip Comstock. "Employee Stock Ownership Plans (ESOPs): Compensation for Whom?" Key Issue No. 23, New York State School of Industrial and Labor Relations, Cornell University, Ithaca, NY, 1978.

Stillwell, Don. "The Devastating Impact of Plant Relocations." *Working Papers for a New Society,* 6, July/August 1978, pp. 42-53.

Wall Street Journal, August 11, 1976.

PART III

WILL COMMUNITY–
EMPLOYEE OWNERSHIP
WORK?

8
Cost-Benefit Methodology and Community Crisis

We must now consider how a community might undertake a similar cost-benefit assessment when faced with the prospect of the closure of a local plant. Which factors are important and how might data be gathered?

Experience in Establishing Employee and Community Owned Firms

There is a rapidly growing number of firms which are employee owned in some manner. Corey Rosen of the Senate Small Business Committee lists some 30 firms, while the study done by Conte and Tannenbaum (1978) found 98 firms with some degree of stock ownership by employees. Thirty of these involved direct stock ownership and 68 had ESOPs. Stern and Hammer (1978a, 1978b) examined fourteen attempts at conversion of threatened U.S. plants to employee or community-employee ownership. In a comparison of eight successful and six unsuccessful conversions, a number of factors emerged which appear critical to success.

The cases listed in table 8-1 show that employee ownership is not restricted to small companies alone. Neither is it restricted to labor intensive industries as some analyses of producers' cooperatives in the U.S. have argued it must be (e.g., Shirom, 1972). Despite the emphasis in this study on the economic decline in the northeastern U.S., the cases also represent a wide geographic distribution. A more complete list of employee owned companies would show even wider geographic dispersion.

197

Table 8-1
Fourteen U.S. Cases of Attempted Conversion to Employee or Community-Employee Ownership

Name	Product	Location	Number of Employees	Successful Acquisition
Library Bureau	Library Furniture	Herkimer, NY	260	Yes
Saratoga Knitting	Yarn Goods	Saratoga, NY	120	Yes
Vermont Asbestos Group	Asbestos	Lowell, VT	178	Yes
Webb's City	Retail Trade	Tampa, FL	450	Yes
South Bend Lathe	Metal Fabricating	South Bend, IN	500	Yes
Chicago and North-western Railroad	Railroad	Chicago, IL	13,000	Yes
Bates Fabrics	Linen	Lewiston, ME	1,100	Yes
Okonite	Wire and Cable	Northern, NJ	1,700	Yes
Universal Atlas	Cement	Hudson, NY	275	No
International Paper	Paper	North Tonawanda, NY	400	No

Hubbard Manufacturing	Metal Fabricating	E. Oakland, CA	100 +	No
Edward Hines	Plywood	Westfir, OR	340	No
Kasanof's	Bake Goods	Boston, MA	285	No
Colonial Press	Printing	Clinton, MA	750-1,800*	No

*At one time this firm employed 1,800 workers but the conglomerate owner Sheller-Globe had laid off workers as business declined.

The process of conversion has four basic components which influence one another: (1) *feasibility study and estimated level of capitalization;* (2) *cost-benefit analysis;* (3) *negotiation with current owner;* and (4) *mobilization of resources.* However, the four components depend upon the existence of entrepreneurial and expert leadership. In successful conversions leadership roles have been played by businessmen, workers, and economic development directors, but such roles have always been critical to the process. The leaders must be capable of organizing resources, providing technical expertise or at least knowing how to obtain the information and skills which are required. In one failed attempt, a production worker who appeared to lead the purchase effort lacked information on how to qualify for government assistance or how the finances of the plant were organized. No economic development officer was available and little local support could be mobilized. The entrepreneurial role is crucial in the complex negotiations which seem to accompany community-employee purchases. In the Herkimer case, John Ladd knew the government regulations and had organizing skills, Richard Rifenburgh was a financial entrepreneur and the managers of the company joined the local effort in providing technical skills.

1. *Feasibility Studies and Capitalization Requirements.* The initial decision to attempt a plant purchase is clearly contingent upon an assessment that the company can be run profitably. Though some might argue that maintaining a plant which is likely to present problems of chronic economic loss is temporarily worthwhile if such a purchase eases the burden upon local labor markets by allowing gradual absorption of workers, a community is unlikely to proceed without good economic prospects. Such studies are, of course, concerned with demand for the company's product, the state of capital goods, debt, and prospective government regulatory requirements along with the ability of the firm to maintain current community income streams, employment levels, and local purchases. Investors will want some idea of potential return on investment and bankers will want the feasibility study as a basis for loan negotiations.

Conventional economic assessments are usually done by management or economic consulting firms that often specialize in particular industries. However, the success or failure of an employee purchase may depend upon specific elements of the assessment which merit special attention.

The financial data required for an adequate feasibility study is often hard to develop, particularly if the current owner is either more interested in a closure than a sale or is hostile to the idea of employee ownership. In Herkimer, the data was available because the former Sperry managers aided the local effort, but the Sperry central office refused to certify the figures and this refusal ultimately restricted the company's ability to sell stock. At the Atlas Cement Plant, U.S. Steel refused to provide any financial data to the local group and most of the management team had already been transferred out of the area. Opposition to the local group was apparently based on the probability that a reopened plant would compete with other U.S. Steel cement facilities and that the local union would supply the financial data to other locals of its international which still bargained with the company (interview with Kenneth Blum, Assistant Plant Superintendent, September 30, 1976). The data necessary for a complete application to either a bank or a government agency was unavailable. Lack of cooperation by the current owner appears to be related to potential competition with the new firm and the importance of the plant's output to other owner production facilities. Plants which are unintegrated, satellite components of a larger corporation should face less difficulty in procuring financial data.

A second critical issue is the required capitalization for the firm. Banks are hesitant when the debt/equity ratio is 3:1 or greater and perceive community-employee ownership as an additional risk. Either negative responses or indecisiveness on the part of private bankers seems largely responsible for the failures at Colonial Press, Hubbard Manufacturing, and perhaps Kasanof's despite feasibility studies suggesting profit potential. An extreme example of the debt/equity problem occurs in the feasibility study undertaken in the massive closings in the Youngstown, Ohio area.

The study investigated reopening of the Campbell Works under community-employee ownership and recommended reopening with a 9:1 debt/equity ratio (National Center for Economic Alternatives, 1978). The amount of capital required is so large that federal intervention on a massive scale would be required.

The debt/equity problem is particularly critical where substantial capital is needed. In Herkimer, the local community contributed nearly two million dollars to establish the firm's equity position. Mechanisms for building or leveraging private investment into larger amounts of capital are required. Federal interest rate subsidies, tax exempt bonds, stock, loan guarantees, and grants have been suggested as equity establishing mechanisms. The Voluntary Job Preservation Act would develop equity capital through loans to employees who would repay such loans through a deduction from wages. The critical nature of this problem is apparent in the successful purchases as well as the failures. In one case the major banking institution involved retained the right to approve the company's choice of chief executive and in another case the company agreed to forego payment of dividends until the initial loans were repaid.

A third rather major issue involves the product market itself. Often an announced closing is preceded by sales cutbacks and refusals to take new orders; former customers may seek alternative suppliers. Loss of market was an apparent problem for the Colonial Press and order cutbacks forced a temporary workforce reduction in Herkimer eight months after the purchase of the plant. Feasibility studies must place importance on the nature of the client-organization relationship. How does the salesforce operate? How much effort will be required to develop or redevelop markets? This issue underscores the importance of early warning of impending closures. Speed is essential in retaining a viable organization. A strong potential for success is highly vulnerable to the loss of clientele during even short disruptions of service.

Some employee groups have found themselves lacking the expertise to make either technical or financial assessments. In addition to raising funds to pay for professional assessments, community groups should seek help from professionals who are willing to contribute services on behalf of community welfare, with reduced fees or in lieu of future considerations. The Economic Development Administration has established several regional technical assistance centers. One such center in Plattsburgh, New York aided in preparation of the Herkimer application to EDA. In the North Tonawanda case, a professor from a nearby university donated his time to assess local forest resources and production processes in the plant. University extension services or faculty willing to assist in exchange for research data should not be overlooked. In still another case, an executive placement service offered to locate and put together a management team without charging normal fees if the new company would agree to use this placement service in the future. A community threatened by economic catastrophe can often obtain help from professionals who are committed either to the community itself or to professional service despite the community's shortage of resources.

2. *Cost-Benefit Analysis.* The feasibility study becomes both an input to a community cost-benefit analysis and a stimulus for it. The study provides information on capital requirements and possible sources of funding, and if its conclusions suggest that the threatened plant has a reasonable probability of operating profitably, a more complete cost-benefit assessment should be made.

Part II of this report illustrates an appropriate cost-benefit methodological model for the assessment. A second model which actually appears to be an impact study rather than an explicit cost-benefit analysis is the "Socioeconomic Costs and Benefits of the Community-Worker Ownership Plan to the Youngstown-Warren SMSA," written by Policy and Management Associates (1978) with respect to the closing of the Campbell Works of Youngstown Sheet and Tube.

Both studies indicate the need for assessments of a wide range of characteristics.

(1) Demography of the area workforce
(2) Labor market conditions
(3) Impacts of closure upon
    (a) employment levels
    (b) local economic base
    (c) personal income
    (d) tax bases
    (e) local purchasing
(4) Local purchases from the plant
(5) Available economic adjustment resources
    (a) unemployment insurance
    (b) trade readjustment assistance
    (c) supplemental unemployment benefits
    (d) severance pay
(6) Mental and physical health impacts
(7) Mobilization potential
(8) Entrepreneurial skill base

The major difficulty in preparing such an evaluation is the gathering of the material needed to construct the document. The problem of firm technical and financial information has already been discussed, but overcoming the resistance of former owners may require the use of political influence as it did in Herkimer. A change in corporate disclosure laws would provide this information.

Several documents are available to assess local demographic and labor market conditions. This study relied heavily upon New York State area labor reports on job openings, hiring specifications, and the unemployed. Many of these documents are available because of U.S. Department of Labor reporting requirements. Much of the Youngstown-Warren study is based on documents from Ohio State Departments of Employment, Economic and Community Development and Taxation. Both studies utilize information provided by area development agencies.

Despite the simplicity of these suggested sources of material, they are worth mentioning because of the events in several of the cases studied. Local businessmen and particularly leaders emerging from among production workers have little knowledge of the vast amount of information provided by state and federal agencies. The group at Atlas Cement knew that local economic conditions were miserable but had no more technical information than that provided by the newspapers until other individuals with appropriate skills and information began to participate in the effort. The owners of Webb's City Department Store complained to their local congressman who directed them to the EDA.

The integration of local, state, and national governments within the current economy means that most local groups will be able to locate appropriate government bodies to obtain information and perhaps assistance. However, time is critical in a threatened closing, and community groups may save time which would be spent searching for required information by developing knowledge of government information services. Researchers and community groups may also benefit from consultation with other research programs, public interest groups, and study centers which have dealt with the issue of plant closings. As the issue of plant closings and employment effects becomes increasingly important, more information and perhaps specific programs will become available.

Suggested Resources

- NATIONAL CENTER FOR ECONOMIC ALTERNATIVES
  2000 P Street NW
  Suite 515
  Washington, DC 20036

This group is largely responsible for the evaluation work on the closing of the Campbell Works of Youngstown Sheet and Tube. The "Socioeconomic Costs and Benefits . . ." study referred to above was done by Policy and Management Associates, Inc. which was working with the center. Another group concerned with plant closings working with the center is Technology Development Inc. which has prepared a report titled "The Public Policy Implications of Plant Closings and Runaways."

- CONFERENCE/ALTERNATIVE STATE AND LOCAL PUBLIC POLICIES
  1901 Q Street NW
  Washington, DC 20009

This group produces resource papers and legislative proposals aimed at changing public policy toward local development and government. One recent paper, "Industrial Exodus," by Edward Kelly, research director of the Ohio Public Interest Campaign, is particularly helpful in discussing public policy strategies for control of the "runaway" plant problem.

In cooperation with the Ohio Public Interest Campaign a report titled "Plant Closings" has been issued. It is a compendium of newspaper and magazine articles along with several position papers. There is a thorough examination of the problem of plant closings and a variety of solutions.

- C&R ASSOCIATES
  Chapel Hill, NC 27514

Rick Carlisle and Michael Redmond have prepared literature review and bibliography with selective annotation on plant closings under contract from the Federal Trade Commission. The paper, "Community Costs of Plant Closings: Bibliography and Survey of the Literature," is a helpful guide to variables which should be considered and gives a detailed comparison of several cases.

- CENTER FOR COMMUNITY ECONOMIC DEVELOPMENT
  639 Massachusetts Avenue
  Room 316
  Cambridge, MA 02139

The center provides research papers and pamphlets which can assist in learning how to utilize federal programs and what community ownership alternatives are available.

- CENTER FOR ECONOMIC STUDIES
  P.O. Box 3736
  Stanford, CA 94305

The center should be able to provide information analyzing the problem of plant shutdowns in terms of the number and impacts of closures.

• The January/February, 1979 issue of the *Public Administration Review* has a symposium on "Policy Analysis in State and Local Government" which includes a short, but helpful, section by Elizabeth David on "Benefit-Cost Analysis in State and Local Investment Decisions."

• NEW SYSTEMS OF WORK AND PARTICIPATION PROGRAM
New York State School of Industrial and Labor Relations
Cornell University
Ithaca, NY 14853

This group can supply research reports on the process of establishing community-employee owned firms, material on current legislation and detailed accounts of the progress of some cases of community-employee or employee ownership.

A list of related groups and topics is provided in Daniel Zwerdling's book *Democracy at Work* published by the Association for Self Management and in an article by Derek Shearer in *Mother Jones* (April, 1978).

3. *Negotiating with the Previous Owner.* Though this topic might not ordinarily merit special attention because it appears on the surface to be a matter of striking a bargain acceptable to both sides in a sales transaction, a community purchase appears to be more complex. First, selling corporations tend to doubt both the managerial and financial ability of community groups. Second, communities usually assemble complex packages for financing purchases in which the entrepreneurial leaders must juggle government agencies, several private banks, and community fund raising all at once. There are numerous points at which difficulties may emerge and selling corporations have tended to set deadlines for sales which create crisis situations for communities. Thus, negotiations become complicated by issues of time limits as well as price. The examples are numerous.

In Herkimer, Sperry Rand demanded a non-refundable deposit, then gave a time limit for the payment of the remaining capital. In this case, the community had to file EDA applications, get bank approvals, and then had 45 days in which to raise 1.8 million dollars through the sale of stock. Three hours before the deadline, the money had not yet been raised, but several arrangements were made to raise the final sum, including a complex loan from the county legislature to the area development corporation. The owner of Kasanof's Bakery decided not to wait beyond a specific date for a required fifty thousand dollar down payment and that effort failed. Similarly, the banks which held the notes on Hubbard Manufacturing decided to auction the plant's equipment rather than wait for the local group to organize itself to raise additional funds. In the establishment of the National Tanning and Trading Corporation, political pressure was used to speed EDA approval of the plan because of deadline pressure applied by the Esmark Corporation which owned the company. Political pressure to extend the deadline for bankruptcy filing by the parent company in the Webb's City case is yet another example.

The negotiations for establishing the community-employee owned firm are often unorthodox and the ability to meet financing package deadlines is an important consideration both in the cost-benefit analysis and the actual implementation of a purchase attempt.

4. *Mobilizing Resources.* The effort which finally determines the outcome of a community-employee purchase attempt is the activity about which economics has much less to say than political science and sociology. The crucial issue is the mobilization of resources, including individuals' time and energy as well as capital. Mobilization of a community to save jobs in a threatened plant closing situation is similar to the resource mobilization task faced by a social movement seeking change. In this case, the change is in the form of ownership of the threatened company.

McCarthy and Zald's elaboration of the resource mobilization strategies of social movements illustrates the community's problem (1977). From the standpoint of those wishing to purchase the plant, the individuals and organizations in the community may be categorized in two ways. They may either be adherents to (believers in) the social movement's goals, or constituents (those who actually contribute to the movement). They may also be divided into beneficiaries or non-beneficiaries (direct and indirect) of the movement's aims. There are likely to be some adversaries to the movement, but the object for members of the movement and movement organizations is to either neutralize these adversaries or convert them to adherents.

Individuals who do not benefit directly from an activity often believe that those who receive the benefits should also bear the costs. Individuals may perceive personal benefit if a plant is saved but simultaneously recognize that these benefits will accrue to them whether they give time and capital or do not. The benefit of saving the plant is a community or public good and some individuals, though adhering to the cause, prefer a "free ride" (Olson, 1968).

In this particular social movement, those actors in the community who actively seek the change in plant ownership must turn adherents and "free riders" into contributing constituents. They must move individuals whose benefits are indirect (the community prospers) to contribute time and capital to the prevention of the plant closing. These individuals are unlikely to lose their own jobs and may not see any personal loss despite the direct loss of jobs suffered by others. The active organizers of the movement must make the issue salient to a large segment of the population, reduce the required individual contribution as much as possible, and make uncommitted individuals feel that their individual contribution to the effort is important.

In Herkimer, television, radio, and newspaper information and advertising were used to make the issue salient. The loss of the plant was pictured as an economic disaster for everyone in the community and the idea of helping neighbors and friends save their jobs, homes, and family was prominent as well. Participation costs were lowered by asking for an investment of only $200 with no commission charges on the sale of stock, and transportation to purchase locations was provided. Contacts were made with individuals who were members of local organizations of all types in order to obtain block support and to increase the use of interpersonal friendship networks as a mechanism for making individual contributions seem important to the effort. In effect, social networks were used to mobilize the community effort. The importance of organizational infrastructure and interpersonal networks has been described by Oberschall (1973) with respect to peasant societies and by Gamson (1975) in examining social protest movements in the U.S.

For the community faced with a shutdown crisis and the potential for community-employee ownership, the resource mobilization perspective suggests several issues which must be addressed in evaluating the possibilities of obtaining community member commitment. The issues involve questions of organizing strategy in planning a fund raising campaign.

(a) Consideration must be given to the composition of the organizing group because the inclusion of business, civic, and social elites with connections to local organizations is crucial. Individuals are needed who are willing to act on behalf of the mobilization effort. They must be the central points in a network of organizations and individuals engaged in raising funds and coordinating information flows.

(b) Potential opponents of the effort should be identified, particularly if they are organizations which are already the focal points of organizational networks. Organized opposition is particularly difficult to overcome when the community is being asked to make a risky financial commitment.

REFERENCES

Conte, Michael and Arnold S. Tannenbaum. *Employee Ownership.* Report to the Economic Development Administration. Ann Arbor, MI: Survey Research Center, 1978.

Freeman, Linton. *Patterns of Community Leadership.* Indianapolis, IN: Bobbs-Merrill, 1968.

Gamson, William. *The Strategy of Social Protest.* Homewood, IL: Dorsey Press, 1975.

Hunter, Floyd. *Community Power Structure.* Garden City, NY: Doubleday, 1953.

Laumann, Edward and Franz Pappi. *Networks of Collective Action.* New York: Academic Press, 1976.

McCarthy, John and Mayer Zald. "Resource Mobilization and Social Movements: A Partial Theory." *American Journal of Sociology,* 82, May 1977, pp. 1212-1242.

National Center for Economic Alternatives. "Youngstown Demonstration Planning Project Summary of Preliminary Findings." Washington: April 11, 1978.

Oberschall, Anthony. *Social Conflict and Social Movements.* Englewood Cliffs, NJ: Prentice-Hall, 1973.

Olson, Mancur Jr. "Economics, Sociology and the Best of All Possible Worlds," *The Public Interest,* 12, Summer 1968, pp. 96-118.

Policy and Management Associates. "Socioeconomic Costs and Benefits of the Community-Worker Ownership Plan to the Youngstown-Warren SMSA," mimeo, 1978.

Shearer, Derek. "Wanna Buy a Used Blast Furnace?" *Mother Jones,* April 1978, pp. 35-52.

Shirom, Arie. "The Industrial Relations Systems of Industrial Cooperatives in the United States, 1880-1935," *Labor History,* Fall 1972, pp. 533-551.

Stern, Robert N. and Tove Helland Hammer. "Buying Your Job: Factors Affecting the Success or Failure of Employee Acquisition Attempts," *Human Relations,* 31, 12, 1978, pp. 1101-1117.

Stern, Robert N. and Tove Helland Hammer. "Buying Your Job: Reconsiderations on Recent Experience." IX World Congress of Sociology. Uppsala, Sweden, August 1978.

Turk, Herman. *Organizations in Modern Life.* San Francisco, CA: Jossey-Bass, Inc., 1977.

Wellman, Barry. "The Community Question: The Intimate Networks of East Yorkers," *American Journal of Sociology,* 84, March 1979, pp. 1201-1232.

9
Prospects for CEFs

The aims of this study have been to evaluate community-employee owned firms as a means of job-saving and to illustrate the methodology for such an evaluation by a community. These aims were pursued primarily through examination of one CEF case—the acquisition of the Library Bureau division of Sperry Rand Corporation by the Mohawk Valley Community Corporation in Herkimer, New York.

The evaluation emphasizes the community viewpoint, but CEFs were also discussed from a societal perspective. The assessment methodology is that of cost-benefit analysis. Both economic and non-economic (sociological, political, psychological, psycho-physiological) variables were taken into account; however, only the economic variables were valued monetarily.

The measure of monetarily valued economic benefits was basically obtained by estimating the difference between the (higher) income stream into the community as a result of the MVCC enabling the plant to continue operations and the income stream if the threatened shutdown had actually occurred. That is, an "avoided cost" concept of benefits was utilized. Non-monetarily valued economic benefits, such as an increase in the community's control of its economic base and likely avoided losses in local government and school district revenue, were also important. This analysis drew heavily upon the literature of regional economics to understand the impact of a manufacturing

213

plant on community income flows and on the findings of labor economics to show likely effects on the displaced employees.

The non-economic factors also largely follow an avoided cost concept. They include avoidance of sociological, psychological, political, and psychophysiological costs which have been directly correlated with job loss and unemployment rates. However, there are additional non-economic benefits derived from mobilizing the local population to establish locally owned rather than absentee owned industry. The community develops itself by increasing its capacity to act in its own behalf. Skills are obtained and new organizations created.

The costs involved are mainly the opportunity costs of the community resources allocated to acquiring and maintaining the MVCC, such as the $1.6 million outlaid for equity capital in the firm.

The ratio of monetarily valued economic benefits to costs is 2.27:1, using the analysis assumptions regarded as most justifiable. The sensitivity of this favorable result to changes in important parameters was considered and the benefit-to-cost ratio remains more than one even when assumptions least favorable to the CEF alternative are employed. The overall evaluation results from the community viewpoint are favorable to the CEF alternative.

From a societal perspective, however, the theoretical framework suggests that the issue is more problematic. Perhaps the core of the problem is whether the capital reallocations involved in plant shutdown decisions by large corporations, acting under the current system of market constraints, are "correct" for the society. There may be market failures, either because firms' capital allocations do not competently adhere to the rule of maximizing internal monetary return, or because this rule is incorrect in not giving significant enough weight to externalities and non-monetized factors. If market failures are judged to exist, then the benefits of appropriate changes must be weighed against the costs. This study has made an exploratory attempt to examine whether there are market failures related to plant closures and is aimed at assessing one means of addressing the possible failures.

Though the general conclusion of the cost-benefit analysis is that community-employee ownership is a viable strategy in plant shutdown situations, the evaluation unfortunately focuses only upon the immediate decision and effort to purchase the plant. A complete examination of CEFs requires a long-run consideration of their economic success and the maintenance of the local autonomy gained through the purchase. Analysis must be done of both the economic success of such firms over time and the development of the communities which purchase the firms. Further, the unique combination of talent and monetary resources available in Herkimer may not be available elsewhere. The situations in which the CEF strategy is applicable may be quite limited.

Two critical questions remain which effect long-run success and community autonomy.

Employee Participation

The examination of employee ownership in chapter 4 argued that productivity gains were available in CEFs because of increased worker commitment to the firm through financial investment and participation in decision making. The increased financial stake is assured by the purchase of stock, but participation through means other than voting one's shares is by no means assured. In fact, shares owned through employee stock ownership plans are not always voted by the stock owners but rather by the trustees of the plan.

Amid the crisis atmosphere of a threatened closing, most individual workers are concerned with saving jobs and not with their decision making rights in the yet to be reborn firm. Forms of organizational control are rarely discussed in such situations (Stern and Hammer, 1978). (However, all control options would be discussed with the purchasing group under the terms of the Job Preservation and Community Stabilization Act.) Furthermore, many workers lack an interest in making decisions on company policy (Locke and Schweiger, 1978; Hammer and Stern, 1980). They have had little practice in decision making and prefer to leave decisions in the hands of expert managers. Gurdon (1978) found that little change in decision making practices occurred in the Saratoga Knitting Mill after the worker purchase.

One cause of this lack of interest in participation is the lack of practice and skill in decision making. Education and practice are needed to promote worker desire for power equalization (Pateman, 1970). Perhaps a greater reason for the minimal interest in change is that the organization is the same one which existed before the crisis, and only the distribution of ownership has changed. The organization falls comfortably into the patterns of past practice. The difficulty, however, is that expectations may have changed while behavior patterns are unaltered. The result after some period of time may be thwarted expectations concerning a partnership among workers, managers, and community members, and pressure for change may result. Recent activity regarding the stock held in trust for workers at the Library Bureau revealed underlying tension concerning the voting of shares. Union officers felt that management was ignoring the fact that the company was employee owned. Labor relations were seen as similar to those which existed under the absentee owner. Failure of management to acknowledge the partnership of management, labor, and community seem to underlie current tension.

Meeting the job threat drew attention away from the implications of spreading ownership to those who usually work only as employees. Changed ownership altered expectations of power sharing, but initially individuals were unsure of their rights as owners, uncertain as to whether they would like to participate in decision making, and thankful that jobs had been saved. Participation may not become organizational practice and the potential benefits available through shared control may be lost. In future cases, a solution to this problem may lie in the introduction of the issue of participation before the plant is actually purchased. The danger of course is that power and control easily become divisive issues and unity of purpose is required to be successful in the purchase attempt.

Retaining Local Control

The strongest social benefit argued for CEFs is the return of control over the economic fate to the local level. Community-employee owned firms must respond to local needs more closely than absentee owned companies do. The difficulty is that success-ful CEFs may not remain locally owned. If community leaders are satisfied with only saving jobs, they may be tempted to return control to outside owners once the crisis is past, or they may see advantages in being part of a larger corporation with greater access to capital and resources to buffer the company against short term adversity.

History provides numerous examples of the difficulty of maintaining local control. Bernstein (1976) describes the problem in his examination of the plywood cooperatives of the U.S. Northwest. The success of the worker owned firm drove up the value of shares in the company. When worker owners reached retirement age, replacement workers could not afford to purchase the highly valued shares. In some cases, large companies from outside the area were the only ones with the capital to purchase shares and companies passed from worker to traditional corporate ownership.

Bernstein determined that after the ownership change: (1) ultimate control over employment and other decisions passed completely out of the communities for which the plants are a major source of employment opportunities; (2) productivity is reported to have decreased; (3) 100 workers were laid off at one plant; and (4) the quality of work is judged by the workers to have declined (1976).

This situation may have occurred because each worker in a cooperative owns only one share of stock, but the loss of control occurs in other ways. Whyte (1978) describes the plight of the Amana community, now the "Amana Corporation."

> As Amana reached the point where its leaders needed large loans in order to expand their facilities to meet potential demand, they were able to get the necessary

credit only through selling out to private investors (p. 74).

The real difficulty is brought closer to the point by an example of a successful job saving purchase by workers at a U.S. Glass Company plant in Tiffin, Ohio in 1963. By pooling resources the workers purchased the plant, refinanced it, and changed the name to Tiffin Art Glass Corporation. Three years later they sold the company to Continental Can which in turn sold it to the Interpace Corporation in 1969 (Kelly, 1977: 20). The Ohio Public Interest Campaign describes this project as the successful saving of 100 jobs through employee purchase.

The description of this "success" identifies the separation of the goals of saving jobs and developing local autonomy. The Tiffin Art Glass Corporation still exists but only at the discretion of a non-local corporation. The community may have developed skills at meeting local crises as well as pride in its ability to defend itself economically, but it has relinquished the degree of control which was gained through local initiative. As long as concern focuses only upon strategies for saving jobs, the long-run ownership of the company may not appear critical, but the financial security of becoming a subsidiary of a large corporation is a trade-off against the vulnerability to corporate policies which subsidiary status brings.

*   *   *

Community-employee ownership is a viable strategy for communities facing plant shutdowns when the plant itself might be made profitable through a change in ownership, some refinancing or limited amounts of new investment. It is a strategy with potential economic and social benefits to local communities including maintenance of economic base and income which may actually induce further economic growth and the development of community skills, pride, and autonomy. However, it is also a strategy with considerable hazards and some difficult costs. Financing is complex and requires coordination of the activities of numerous individuals, local organizations, and government agencies. The saving of jobs and the development of local economic control are somewhat independent, however, and local control seems to be fragile once the crisis is past.

Beyond recognizing that the CEF strategy is viable, this study should also emphasize that the strategy is only appropriate in limited situations. It requires that communities carefully evaluate the economic prospects of threatened firms and turn to other forms of easing the impact of plant closings when the local company is in fact economically disadvantaged.

REFERENCES

Bernstein, Paul. *Workplace Democratization: Its Internal Dynamics.* Kent, OH: Kent State University, 1976.

Gurdon, Michael A. *The Structure of Ownership: Implications for Employee Influence in Organizational Design.* Unpublished Doctoral Dissertation, New York State School of Industrial and Labor Relations, Cornell University, 1978.

Kelly, Edward. *Industrial Exodus: Public Strategies for Control of Runaway Plants.* Washington: Conference/Alternative State and Local Public Policies, October 1977, p. 20.

Locke, E.A. and S.M. Schweiger. "Participation in Decision-Making— One More Look," in *Research in Organizational Behavior,* Vol. I, B.M. Staw, ed. Greenwich, CT: JAI Press, 1978.

Pateman, Carole. *Participation and Democratic Theory.* London: Cambridge University Press, 1970.

Stern, Robert N. and Tove Helland Hammer. "Buying Your Job: Factors Affecting the Success or Failure of Employee Acquisition Attempts," *Human Relations,* 31, 1978, pp. 1101-1117.

Whyte, William Foote. "In Support of Voluntary Employee Ownership," *Society,* 15, 6, September/October 1978, pp. 73-82.

Date Due

BRODART, INC.

233   Printed in U.S.A